Science

The 13+ Study Book

For the Common Entrance 13+ exams

How to get your free Online Edition

Just go to **cgpbooks.co.uk/extras** and enter this code...

1676 1564 5074 7294

By the way, this code only works for one person. If somebody else has used this book before you, they might have already claimed the Online Edition.

Practise • Prepare • Pass

Everything your child needs for 13+ success

CONTENTS

Published by CGP

Editors:
Charlotte Burrows, Mary Falkner, Gordon Henderson, Sam Pilgrim, Rachael Rogers
and Sophie Scott.

With thanks to Ian Francis, Sue Hunter and Karen Wells for the reviewing and proofreading.

With thanks to Laura Jakubowski for the copyright research.

Data used to construct stopping distance diagram on page 84 From the Highway Code.
© Crown Copyright re-produced under the terms of the Open Government licence
http://www.nationalarchives.gov.uk/doc/open-government-licence/

Image on page 100 © iStockphoto.com/3DSculptor.

ISBN: 978 1 78294176 7

Printed by Elanders Ltd, Newcastle upon Tyne.
Clipart from Corel®

13+ Science

Like it or not, you're going to be tested on 13+ Science at some point.
At least this page should shed some light on what to expect come exam day...

There are **Two Levels** in the **13+ Science** Exams

1) You can either do <u>Level 1</u> or <u>Level 2</u> exams for <u>Common Entrance 13+ Science</u> (the Level 2 exams are a bit harder).

2) The exam papers are structured <u>differently</u> for each level.

3) There's only <u>one paper</u> for the <u>Level 1</u> exam, and it tests you on all three science subjects (Biology, Chemistry and Physics).

4) There are <u>three separate papers</u> for the <u>Level 2</u> exam — one for each of the three sciences.

5) The number of <u>marks</u> and the amount of <u>time</u> you get is different for each level, as shown in these <u>handy diagrams</u>:

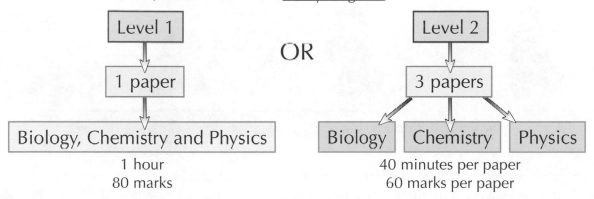

OR

Level 1 → 1 paper → Biology, Chemistry and Physics
1 hour
80 marks

Level 2 → 3 papers → Biology, Chemistry, Physics
40 minutes per paper
60 marks per paper

You Might Sit the **CASE Paper**

1) You may be entered for the <u>CASE paper</u> — CASE stands for <u>C</u>ommon <u>A</u>cademic <u>S</u>cholarship <u>E</u>xamination. You'll be <u>told</u> if you're sitting this paper.

2) The CASE exam paper lasts for <u>1 hour 30 minutes</u> and is worth <u>75 marks</u>.

3) There are <u>three</u> sections in the exam — one for each of <u>Biology</u>, <u>Chemistry</u> and <u>Physics</u>.

If your school sets its own 13+ exams, the paper might be a bit different to what's described on this page. Ask your teacher what your papers will look like.

All the Exams Test You on **How Science Works**

1) <u>Whichever exam</u> you're doing, <u>some</u> of the questions on the paper will test your knowledge of <u>How Science Works</u>.

2) You'll learn a lot of what you need to know about this from the <u>practical investigations</u> you do in class, plus there's a <u>whole section</u> on How Science Works coming up next (see pages 2-6).

3) There are loads of ways the examiners could test your knowledge of this stuff. For example, you might be asked to draw a <u>graph</u> of some results, <u>analyse some data</u>, make a <u>conclusion</u> or maybe <u>evaluate</u> a <u>method</u> that was used for an experiment.

In both the Level 2 Common Entrance and the CASE paper, at least 25% of the exam will test How Science Works.

Testing, testing, one two, one two...

This book is up and running and hopefully you're hearing me loud and clear. There's lots on How Science Works over the next few pages. Make sure you learn this as well as all of the 'regular science'.

How Science Works

The Scientific Process

Scientists work scientifically — it's their job. It means they can plan awesome investigations, get useful results and draw scientific conclusions from them. You need to be able to do all that too. Fear not though, this section will tell you everything you need to know.

A **Hypothesis** is an **Explanation** of Something

1) Scientists <u>observe</u> (look at) things they <u>don't understand</u>.
2) They then come up with an <u>explanation</u> for what they've seen.
3) This explanation is called a <u>hypothesis</u>.

> **Example:**
>
> A scientist is looking at <u>why</u> people have <u>spots</u>.
>
>
>
> He notices that everyone with spots <u>picks their nose</u>.
>
>
>
> The scientist thinks that the spots might be <u>caused</u> by people picking their nose.
>
>
>
> Nose picking = spots?
>
> So the <u>hypothesis</u> is: "Spots are caused by picking your nose."

4) Next, scientists need to <u>check</u> whether the <u>hypothesis</u> is <u>right or not</u>.
5) They do this by making a <u>prediction</u> and <u>testing</u> it.

You need to be able to make predictions too.

> **Example:**
>
> A prediction is something like: "People who pick their nose will have spots."

6) If tests show that the <u>prediction</u> is <u>right</u>, then there's <u>evidence</u> (signs) that the <u>hypothesis is right</u> too.
7) If tests show that the <u>prediction</u> is <u>wrong</u>, then the <u>hypothesis</u> is probably <u>wrong</u> as well.

Other Scientists *Test* the *Hypothesis*

1) It's <u>not enough</u> for <u>one scientist</u> to do tests to see if the hypothesis is right or not.
2) That's why scientists <u>publish</u> their <u>results</u> — so <u>other scientists</u> can find out about the hypothesis and do the <u>tests</u> for themselves. Results are published in <u>peer-reviewed journals</u>.
3) Sometimes other scientists will find <u>more evidence</u> that the <u>hypothesis is right</u>.
4) When this happens, the hypothesis is <u>accepted</u> and goes into <u>books</u> for people to learn. An accepted hypothesis is often called a <u>theory</u>.

> A <u>journal</u> is a collection of scientific papers. '<u>Peer-reviewed</u>' means other scientists have checked the results and scientific explanations before the journal is published.

5) Sometimes the scientists will find <u>evidence</u> that shows the <u>hypothesis is wrong</u>.
6) When this happens, scientists have to either <u>change</u> the hypothesis or come up with a <u>new one</u>.
7) Sometimes <u>new evidence</u> will be found that means an <u>accepted theory</u> needs to <u>change</u>. This is how theories <u>develop</u>.

Investigations

Scientists do investigations to find things out. You need to be able to do investigations too...

Investigations *Give Us* Evidence

1) Scientists carry out <u>investigations</u> to <u>test</u> their <u>predictions</u> and collect <u>evidence</u> to <u>back up their ideas</u>.
2) <u>You</u> need to be able to <u>plan</u> and <u>carry out investigations</u> to test <u>your predictions</u>.
3) You can do investigations in a <u>lab</u> (laboratory) or <u>somewhere else</u>. For example:
   - A <u>lab</u> is the best place to study most <u>chemical reactions</u>.
   - But if you want to know how many <u>rabbits</u> there are in a wood, you'll need to <u>go outside</u>. This is called <u>fieldwork</u>... although it doesn't always have to be done in a field.

Investigations *Have to be* Fair Tests

1) Before you start an investigation, you need to <u>plan</u> what you're going to do.
2) You need to <u>make sure</u> your investigation will really <u>test</u> whether your prediction is <u>right</u> or <u>not</u>.
3) To do this, you must make sure it will be a <u>fair test</u>. This means you must...

> <u>Only change one thing</u>. <u>Everything else</u> must be kept the <u>same</u>.

4) The thing that you <u>change</u> is called the <u>INDEPENDENT</u> variable.
5) The things that you <u>keep the same</u> are called <u>CONTROL</u> variables.
6) The <u>effect</u> that's <u>measured</u> is called the <u>DEPENDENT</u> variable.

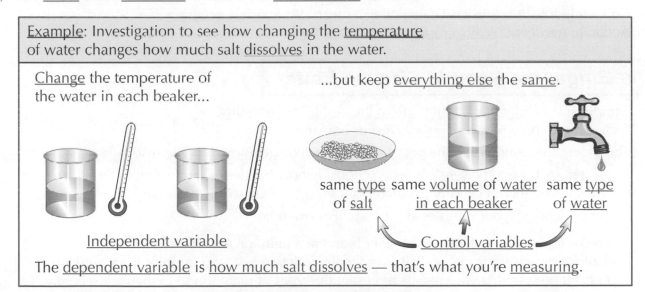

<u>Example</u>: Investigation to see how changing the <u>temperature</u> of water changes how much salt <u>dissolves</u> in the water.

<u>Change</u> the temperature of the water in each beaker...

...but keep <u>everything else</u> the <u>same</u>.

same <u>type</u> of <u>salt</u>   same <u>volume</u> of <u>water</u> in each beaker   same <u>type</u> of <u>water</u>

Independent variable   Control variables

The <u>dependent variable</u> is <u>how much salt dissolves</u> — that's what you're <u>measuring</u>.

The *Equipment Has to be* Right for the Job

1) You need to choose the <u>right equipment</u> for your investigation.
2) For example, choose <u>measuring equipment</u> that will let you measure stuff <u>accurately</u>.

If you need to measure out <u>11 ml</u>, this measuring cylinder would be great. It's the <u>right size</u> and you can <u>see</u> where 11 ml is.

This measuring cylinder isn't as good. It's <u>too big</u> and you <u>can't really see</u> where 11 ml is.

How Science Works

Investigations

Investigations Can be **Hazardous**

1) A hazard is something that could cause harm — e.g. bacteria, chemicals, electricity and fire.
2) Scientists need to manage the risk of hazards by doing things to reduce them.
   For example, if you're using a Bunsen burner:

> • Stand it on a heat-proof mat. This will reduce the risk of starting a fire.
>
> • Always turn it off or to the yellow safety flame when you're not using it.
>
> • Keep any flammable substances (like ethanol) away from the flame.
>
> • Wear goggles to protect your eyes — liquids can spit when they boil, and there's
>   always a risk that glassware (test tubes etc.) might shatter when you heat it.

Investigations Need to be **Repeated**

1) The more times you repeat your investigation the better — but three times is usually enough.
   Then you can work out the mean (average) — see next page.
2) If you get the same or very similar results each time you repeat your
   investigation, that's good news. It means your results are repeatable.
3) It also means they're more likely to be reproducible by other scientists.
   If other scientists can reproduce your results, it's more likely that your hypothesis is right (see p. 2).
4) Results that are both repeatable and reproducible are said to be reliable.
5) Collecting lots of results and calculating a mean can improve accuracy.
   Accurate results are really close to the true answer.

The **Bigger** the **Sample Size** the **Better**

1) Sample size is how many things are in the group you're testing.
   For example, how many plants you test or how many people.
2) The bigger the sample size the better — it means you get more reliable results.
3) But scientists have to be sensible when choosing how big their sample should be. If it's too small,
   their results might not be very accurate. If it's too big the investigation might take ages to do.
4) It's best to choose your samples at random. For example:

   If you're investigating the types of plant found in a field, divide the field into a grid and take
   samples from random squares, all over the field. If you just take samples from one corner,
   you can't be sure that your results represent the types of plant found in the whole field.

Errors Can Pop Up if You're **Not Careful**

1) The results of your experiment will always vary a bit because of random errors
   — tiny differences caused by things like making a mistake when you're measuring.
2) If the same error is made every time, it's called a systematic error. For example...

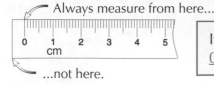

Always measure from here...

...not here.

> If you measure from the very end of your ruler instead of from the
> 0 cm mark every time, all your measurements would be a bit small.

Organising and Presenting Data

Once you've collected your data (results) you need to organise and present them nice and clearly.

Data Needs to be *Organised* so it can be *Processed* Later On

1) Tables are dead useful for organising data.
2) You should always make sure that each column has a heading and that you've included the units.

Test tube	Volume of gas produced (cm³)		
	Repeat 1	Repeat 2	Repeat 3
A	28	37	32
B	47	51	60
C	68	72	70

You Might Have to *Process Your Data*

1) When you've done repeats of an experiment you should always calculate the mean (average).
2) To calculate the mean add together all the data values, then divide by the total number of data values.

Test tube	Mass (g)				
	Repeat 1	Repeat 2	Repeat 3	Mean	Range
A	28	37	32	$(28 + 37 + 32) \div 3 = 32.3$	$37 - 28 = 9$
B	47	51	60	$(47 + 51 + 60) \div 3 = 52.7$	$60 - 47 = 13$

3) You might also need to calculate the range (how spread out the data is).
4) To do this find the largest number and subtract the smallest number from it.
5) You want your results to be as precise (close to the mean) as possible — so the smaller the range, the better your results.

You Can *Present* Your *Data* in a *Graph* or *Bar Chart*

1) Presenting data in a graph or bar chart makes it easier to spot patterns in the results (see next page).
2) Make sure axes on your graphs and charts have a sensible scale, are labelled and include the units.

Bar Charts

1) If you're measuring something that comes in categories you should use a bar chart to show the data.
2) Categories are things like type of nutrient or blood group. You can't get results in-between categories.

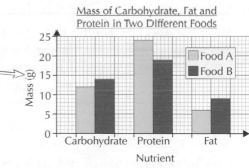

Mass of Carbohydrate, Fat and Protein in Two Different Foods

Line Graphs

1) If you're measuring something that can have any value (e.g. temperatures and people's heights) you should use a line graph to show the data.
2) The dependent variable (the thing you measure) goes on the y-axis.
3) The independent variable (the thing you change) goes on the x-axis.
4) You can draw a line of best fit (or a curve of best fit if your points make a curve) — a line that goes through or as near to as many of the points as possible.
5) You can use a line of best fit to estimate values for readings you didn't take during the experiment. This value might not be accurate if you extend the line beyond your data points.

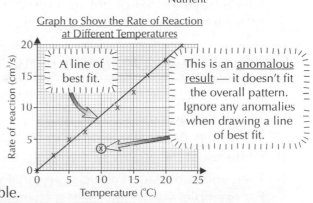

Graph to Show the Rate of Reaction at Different Temperatures

A line of best fit.

This is an anomalous result — it doesn't fit the overall pattern. Ignore any anomalies when drawing a line of best fit.

Concluding and Evaluating

Drawing a conclusion is all about finding patterns in your data.

Line Graphs Can Show Patterns in Data

1) When you're carrying out an investigation it's not enough to just present your data — you've also got to find any <u>patterns</u> in the data.

2) Line graphs are great for showing patterns in data.

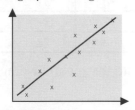

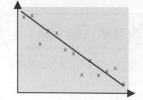

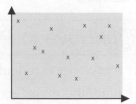

You can see here that as one variable <u>increases</u> the other <u>increases</u> too.

Here, as one variable <u>increases</u> the other <u>decreases</u>.

There's absolutely <u>no</u> <u>pattern</u> to be seen here...

A Conclusion is a Summary of What You've Learnt

1) Once you've organised and presented your data, you need to analyse it and come to a <u>conclusion</u>.

2) You just have to <u>look at your data</u> and <u>say what pattern you see</u>.

<u>EXAMPLE</u>: The table shows how tall pea plants grew with different fertilisers.

Fertiliser	Mean growth / mm
A	13.5
B	19.5
C	5.5

<u>CONCLUSION</u>:
Fertiliser <u>B</u> makes
<u>pea plants</u> grow taller
than fertiliser A or
fertiliser C.

Fertiliser B
Winner!

3) You also need to use the data that's been <u>collected</u> to <u>justify</u> the conclusion (back it up).

<u>EXAMPLE continued</u>: On average, fertiliser B made the pea plants grow 6 mm
taller than fertiliser A and 14 mm taller than fertiliser C.

4) You should also use your own <u>scientific knowledge</u> (the stuff you've learnt in class) to try to <u>explain</u> the conclusion.

5) Finally, say whether or not your results <u>back up</u> your original <u>hypothesis</u> — or say whether your original <u>prediction</u> was <u>right or wrong</u>.

Evaluation — Describe How It Could be Improved

In an evaluation you look back over the whole investigation.

1) You should comment on the <u>method</u> — did it produce <u>reliable</u> results? If not, why not? Were there any potential sources of <u>error</u>?

2) Write about the <u>quality</u> of the <u>results</u> too — were they <u>repeatable</u> and <u>accurate</u>?

3) Then you can suggest any <u>changes</u> that would <u>improve</u> the quality of the results. For example, you might suggest changing the way you controlled a variable.

4) Your results might give you ideas for <u>further investigations</u> too. For example, you might come up with a <u>new question</u> that needs answering. Then the whole <u>scientific process</u> starts again...

Cells

This page is about what living things are made of. Prepare to find out that you're quite similar to a plant.

Living Things are Made of *Cells*

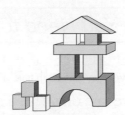

1) Another word for a <u>living thing</u> is an <u>organism</u>. <u>All organisms</u> are made up of <u>tiny building blocks</u> known as <u>cells</u>.

2) You need to know the different <u>components</u> that make up <u>animal cells</u> and <u>plant cells</u>.

Animal and *Plant Cells* Have *Similarities* and *Differences*

An *Animal* Cell

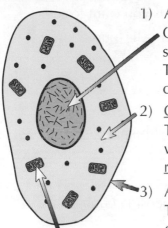

A *Plant* Cell

BOTH have:

1) A <u>nucleus</u>:
Contains genes, which are sections of DNA (see p. 29). The genes <u>control</u> what the cell <u>does</u>.

2) Cytoplasm:
This is a jelly-like stuff where most <u>chemical reactions</u> happen.

3) A <u>cell surface membrane</u>:
This is a thin skin around the cell. It <u>holds the cell together</u> and <u>controls</u> what goes <u>in and out</u>.

4) <u>Mitochondria</u>:
These are tiny structures inside the cell where most of the reactions for <u>aerobic respiration</u> (see p. 10) take place. Respiration <u>releases energy</u> for the cell.

ONLY PLANTS have:

1) A <u>cell wall</u>:
A rigid outer coating made of <u>cellulose</u> — it gives <u>support</u> to the cell.

2) A <u>permanent vacuole</u>:
This is filled with <u>cell sap</u> — a weak solution of sugar and salts.

3) <u>Chloroplasts</u>:
These contain <u>chlorophyll</u> used for <u>photosynthesis</u> (see p. 24). Photosynthesis <u>makes food</u> for the plant.

Learn *How Cells* are *Organised*

1) <u>Animals</u> and <u>plants</u> are made up of <u>lots of cells</u> — they're <u>multicellular</u> organisms.

2) In organisms with <u>lots of cells</u>, the cells are <u>organised</u> into <u>groups</u>. Here's how:

> A group of <u>similar cells</u> come together to make a <u>tissue</u>.
> A group of <u>different tissues</u> work together to make an <u>organ</u>.

EXAMPLE:
- <u>Muscle cells</u> make up <u>muscle tissue</u>.
- <u>Muscle tissue</u>, with <u>other tissues</u>, makes up the <u>heart</u> (an <u>organ</u>).

Cells — they're great for locking things up...

You need to learn what all the parts of an animal cell and a plant cell are called and what they do. Have a good read of the page, then cover it up and try drawing and labelling the two cells above. Keep going until you're sure about all the different bits. It's the best way to get it stuck in your head.

The Microscope

A microscope magnifies really tiny objects (makes them look bigger) so you can see them. Clever stuff. You need to know how to use a microscope to look at plant and animal cells.

Firstly You Need to **Prepare** a **Microscope Slide**

1) A microscope slide is a strip of clear glass or plastic with the material that you want to look at (e.g. cells) stuck to it.

2) To prepare one, take a small sample of the cells you want to look at. Place it in the middle of a clean microscope slide.

3) Use a pipette (dropper) to add a drop of water or a stain (see below) to the sample.

4) Carefully put a clean coverslip (a small, thin piece of plastic or glass) over the top. Then you're ready to look at your cells under the microscope.

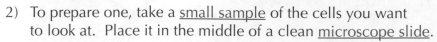

1) Adding a stain (dye) to cells on a microscope slide makes it easier to see the cell parts.

2) You need to use different stains depending on which bits of the cells you want to see.

3) For example, the stain methylene blue colours the nuclei of animal cells blue.

You Can Use a **Microscope** to Look at **Cells**

Here are the main parts of a light microscope — make sure you can identify them.

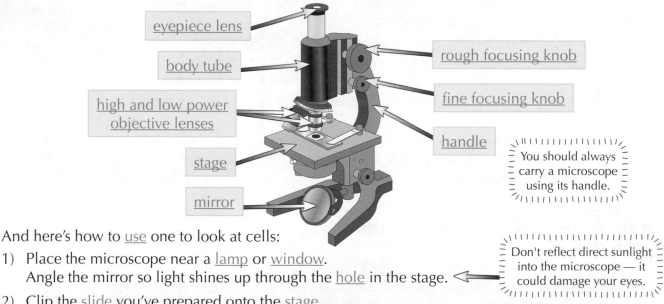

eyepiece lens

body tube

high and low power objective lenses

stage

mirror

rough focusing knob

fine focusing knob

handle

> You should always carry a microscope using its handle.

> Don't reflect direct sunlight into the microscope — it could damage your eyes.

And here's how to use one to look at cells:

1) Place the microscope near a lamp or window. Angle the mirror so light shines up through the hole in the stage.

2) Clip the slide you've prepared onto the stage.

3) Select the lowest powered objective lens.

4) Turn the rough focusing knob to move the objective lens down to just above the slide.

5) Look down the eyepiece lens and adjust the focus using the fine focusing knob. Keep adjusting until you get a clear image of the cells on the slide.

6) If you need to see the cells with greater magnification, switch to a higher powered objective lens and refocus the microscope (repeat steps 4 and 5).

Microscopes — useful for looking at onions...

Teachers just love getting you to look through a microscope at the slimy skin between the layers of an onion (yuk). A microscope lets you see the cells that the onion skin is made up of. It's interesting stuff.

Specialised Cells

All living things carry out the same life processes — things like movement, reproduction and nutrition. Many plant and animal cells have special features (adaptations) to help them carry out these functions. We call these cells 'specialised cells' — this page gives you four examples...

Ciliated Epithelial Cells can Move Particles

1) Epithelial cells cover the surfaces of your body. For example, the skin and the gut lining are both made up of epithelial cells.

2) Some epithelial cells have tiny hair-like structures called cilia sticking out from them.

3) Cells like these are called ciliated epithelial cells.

4) Cilia can beat — this means that they all move in the same direction at the same time. This beating motion can move particles in a certain direction.

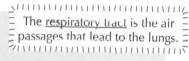

cilia

epithelial cell

EXAMPLE

1) Your respiratory tract is lined with ciliated epithelial cells. It's also coated in a layer of lovely sticky mucus.

2) Any dust particles or bacteria that you breathe in get trapped in the mucus.

3) The beating of the cilia carries the mucus upwards and out of the respiratory tract.

The respiratory tract is the air passages that lead to the lungs.

Ova and Sperm are Specialised For Reproduction

The ovum (egg cell) and sperm are the female and male cells involved in animal reproduction (see p. 18).

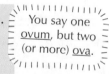

ovum (egg cell)

1) The ovum carries the female DNA in its nucleus.

2) It contains a food store to nourish (feed) a developing embryo in its early stages.

You say one ovum, but two (or more) ova.

There's more about ova and sperm on pages 16 and 18.

sperm

1) The function of a sperm is to get the male DNA to the ovum.

2) It has a long tail to help it swim to the ovum.

3) There are lots of mitochondria (see p. 7) in the cell to provide the energy it needs to do this.

4) Sperm also carry enzymes in their heads to help them break through the cell membrane of the ovum.

Root Hair Cells Absorb Water and Minerals From the Soil

1) The cells on the surface of plant roots grow into long "hairs" which stick out into the soil.

2) This gives the plant a big surface area for absorbing water and minerals from the soil.

3) Root hair cells also have thin cell walls — this makes it easier for water and minerals to get into the cell.

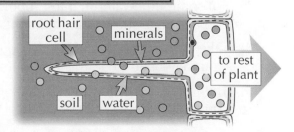

root hair cell

minerals

to rest of plant

soil

water

Flying saucers, tadpoles — cells are masters of disguise...

These cells look very different — that's because they have their own special features that help them to do their jobs. See if you can draw each cell on this page and describe how it's adapted to its function.

Respiration

As life processes go, this is the big one — respiration. Without it, you'd be well and truly stuck.

Respiration is a Chemical Reaction

1) Respiration happens in <u>every cell</u> of <u>every living organism</u>.

2) Respiration is the process of <u>releasing energy</u> from <u>glucose</u> (a sugar).

3) The energy released by respiration is used for <u>all the other chemical reactions</u> that keep you <u>alive</u>.
For example, the reactions involved in:

<u>building</u>
<u>proteins</u>

<u>muscle</u>
<u>contraction</u>

<u>keeping</u>
<u>warm</u>

Aerobic Respiration Needs Plenty of Oxygen

1) <u>Aerobic respiration</u> is respiration using <u>oxygen</u>. It takes place in the <u>mitochondria</u> (see page 7) of <u>animal</u> and <u>plant cells</u>.

There's another type of respiration that can happen without oxygen, but you don't need to know about it here.

2) In aerobic respiration, <u>glucose</u> and <u>oxygen</u> react to produce <u>carbon dioxide</u> and <u>water</u>. This reaction releases <u>lots of energy</u>.

3) Here's the <u>word equation</u> to show what happens in this reaction — <u>learn it</u>:

glucose + oxygen ⟶ carbon dioxide + water + ENERGY

These are the <u>reactants</u>.   These are the <u>products</u>.

There's more on word equations on page 44.

4) <u>Glucose</u> comes from your <u>food</u>. It's carried to cells in your <u>bloodstream</u>.

5) <u>Oxygen</u> comes from the <u>air</u>. When you <u>breathe in</u>, oxygen from the air enters your <u>blood</u> at the <u>lungs</u> and is carried to your cells (see page 19).

6) <u>Blood</u> also carries <u>carbon dioxide</u> away from your cells — it goes back to your lungs to be <u>breathed out</u> (<u>exhaled</u>).

Use Limewater to Test Exhaled Air For Carbon Dioxide

You can show that <u>exhaled air</u> contains <u>carbon dioxide</u> by doing an experiment using limewater.
<u>Limewater</u> is a <u>colourless</u> solution — but it turns <u>cloudy</u> when you bubble <u>carbon dioxide</u> through it.

This is how you do the experiment:

1) Put some limewater in a test tube.
Pop a <u>tube</u> (a straw will do) into it.

2) Take a deep breath and <u>breathe out</u> into the tube.
(You may need to do this a few times.)

3) The limewater will turn <u>cloudy</u>, showing that the air you are breathing out contains <u>carbon dioxide</u>.

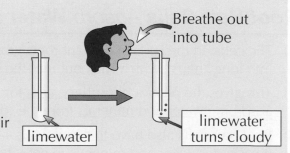

Breathe out
into tube

limewater

limewater
turns cloudy

Respiration — it's energetic stuff...

It can be hard getting to grips with the idea of respiration, but it just means turning glucose into energy.
Respiration is not the same as breathing — breathing is moving air in and out of the lungs (see p. 19).

Summary Questions

Welcome to your very first page of summary questions. It's full of questions written especially for finding out what you actually know — and, more importantly, what you don't. Here's what you have to do...
1) Go through the whole lot of questions and try to answer them. 2) Look up the answers to any you can't do and try to really learn them (hint: the answers are all somewhere in Section 1). 3) Try all the questions again to see if you can answer more than you could before. 4) Keep going till you get them all right. Ready? Off you go then...

1) What is an organism?

2) Name four parts that both plant cells and animal cells have. Say what they all do.

3) Name three parts of a cell that only plant cells have.

4) What term is used for an organism that is made up of lots of cells?

5) Explain the meaning of: a) a tissue,
   b) an organ.

6) Briefly describe how you would prepare a microscope slide of a sample.

7) Why might you add a stain to a microscope slide?

8) Give an example of a stain. Say which bit of the cell the stain is used to highlight.

9) What part of a microscope do you clip your slide onto?

10) What job should you use the rough focusing knob on a microscope for?
    What about the fine focusing knob?

11) What are cilia?

12) Explain why your respiratory tract is lined with ciliated epithelial cells.

13) Give one way that an ovum is adapted to its function.

14) a) Name two ways that a sperm cell is adapted for swimming to an egg cell.
    b) Give one other way in which a sperm cell is adapted to its function.

15) a) Draw a simple diagram to show the shape of a root hair cell. Why is it this shape?
    b) How is the cell wall of a root hair cell adapted to help the cell perform its function?

16) What's the name of the process that goes on in every cell, releasing energy?

17) Write down the word equation for aerobic respiration.

18) Where does the glucose that your cells use for respiration come from?
    How does it get to your cells?

19) Briefly describe how the gas that your body makes during respiration
    gets from your cells into the air.

20) a) What happens to limewater when carbon dioxide is bubbled through it?
    b) Describe an experiment that you could do to show that exhaled air
       contains carbon dioxide.

Section 1 — Cells and Respiration

Nutrition

Nutrition is all about getting the food and drink you need to stay healthy.
A balanced diet will have the right amount of the five nutrients listed below, as well as fibre and water.

1) Carbohydrates

E.g. starch, glucose　　Bread / potatoes / cereals　　Energy

These are like fuel for your body — your body uses glucose molecules in respiration to release all the energy you need to keep you going (see page 10).

You can test whether starch is present in a food using the iodine test (see page 25).

2) Proteins

Proteins　　Meat / eggs / fish　　Building Cells

Proteins are vital for growth and to repair damaged areas.

3) Fats

Fat　　Butter / cooking oil / cream　　Energy

Fats act as a store of energy, which you use if your body runs out of carbohydrates. Stored fats also act as insulation to keep you warm.

4) Vitamins

E.g. A B₁ B₂ C D E

Vegetables / fruit / cereals

Vitamins are only needed in very small amounts — they keep many vital processes happening.

5) Minerals

E.g. —	Iron	Calcium salts	Sodium
Found in —			
Needed for –	Blood	Teeth/Bones	Nerves

Fibre

Vegetables / fruit / cereals

Fibre helps food move through your digestive system.

Water

About 75% of your body is water and all chemical reactions (e.g. digestion), take place in water – it's well important!

Obviously we only had gruel when I was a lad... sob... sob...

Five types of nutrient, what you find them in and what they're for. And then there's fibre and water too.
Learn each section and test yourself with the one method that works — covering the page and writing it out.

Staying Healthy

Making sure you have a balanced diet and enough exercise is really important for keeping you healthy.

An *Unbalanced Diet* Can Cause *Health Problems*

Problems Can be Caused by *Not Getting Enough* of Something...

Some people don't get enough <u>vitamins or minerals</u> — this can cause <u>diseases</u>.

Example 1 — Lack of Vitamin C

1) <u>Vitamin C</u> is found in loads of <u>fruits</u> and <u>vegetables</u> such as oranges, strawberries, peppers and broccoli.

2) A lack of <u>vitamin C</u> can cause <u>scurvy</u>, a disease that causes problems with the <u>skin</u>, <u>joints</u> and <u>gums</u>.

Example 2 — Lack of Calcium

1) <u>Calcium</u> is found in foods such as <u>dairy products</u> and <u>leafy green vegetables</u>.

2) A lack of calcium in the diet can contribute to the development of <u>osteoporosis</u> — a disease in which the <u>bones</u> become <u>less dense</u> and are more likely to <u>fracture</u>.

...or by Getting *Too Much*

Too much energy

1) If you <u>take in more energy</u> from your diet <u>than you use up</u>, your body will store the <u>extra energy</u> as <u>fat</u> — so you will <u>put on weight</u>.

2) If you weigh <u>over 20% more</u> than the recommended weight for your height, then you are classed as <u>obese</u>.

3) Obesity can lead to <u>health problems</u> such as <u>high blood pressure</u> and <u>heart disease</u>.

Too much saturated fat

1) <u>Animal products</u> that contain <u>fat</u> (e.g. cheese, cream, butter) tend to have a high proportion of <u>saturated fat</u>.

2) Having <u>too much</u> saturated fat in your diet can increase your <u>blood cholesterol level</u>.

3) Having a <u>high</u> blood cholesterol level increases the risk of <u>heart disease</u>.

Cholesterol is a fatty substance that's essential for good health — it's found in every cell in the body.

Exercise is Important for *Staying Healthy*

1) <u>Exercise</u> is important as well as diet — people who exercise regularly are usually <u>healthier</u> than those who don't.

2) Exercise increases the amount of energy <u>used</u> by the body and decreases the amount <u>stored as fat</u>. So people who exercise are <u>less likely</u> to suffer from <u>obesity</u>.

3) Exercise can also <u>reduce the risk</u> of many other health problems such as <u>heart disease</u>, some <u>cancers</u> and <u>depression</u>.

4) It can also <u>build muscle</u>, increase <u>energy levels</u> and improve <u>coordination</u> — crikey, it's good.

You'll go all wobbly if your diet isn't balanced...

You need to know why it's important that you get enough vitamin C and calcium in your diet and why you should go easy on animal fats. You need to know why exercise is important for staying healthy too.

Digestion

Digestion is All About Breaking Down Food

1) In digestion, the digestive system breaks down food we eat, so we can use the nutrients it contains.

2) Digestion involves digestive enzymes. Enzymes are molecules which speed up chemical reactions, so digestive enzymes help to speed up the chemical reactions which break down food (see below).

Seven Bits of The Digestive System

1) Mouth

Digestion starts here where the teeth have a good old chew and mix the food with saliva. Saliva contains digestive enzymes.

4) Liver

The liver makes bile, which breaks fats up into tiny droplets.

6) Large intestine

Water is absorbed here.

7) Rectum

Waste materials of digestion are stored here as faeces (poo). Eventually they are egested from the anus.

2) Stomach

Here the food gets churned up and mixed with more digestive enzymes.

3) Pancreas

The pancreas produces lots of digestive enzymes, which are released into the small intestine.

5) Small intestine

1) This produces more enzymes.

2) It is lined with tiny finger-like projections called villi — these increase the surface area of the small intestine.

3) Food molecules are absorbed into the blood across the villi.

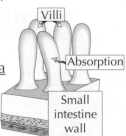
Villi
Absorption
Small intestine wall

The small intestine is sometimes called the gut.

Absorption of Food Molecules

1) Big, insoluble food molecules can't pass through the gut wall.

2) So enzymes are used to break up big molecules into smaller, soluble ones.

3) For example, amylase is an enzyme that's involved in breaking down starch into simple sugars:

'Insoluble' means 'won't dissolve'. 'Soluble' means 'will dissolve'. See page 46.

starch → amylase → simple sugars

4) The small molecules produced by enzyme action can pass through the gut wall into the blood. They are then carried round the body, before passing into cells to be used.

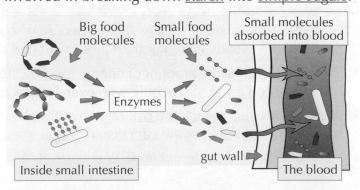
Big food molecules
Small food molecules
Small molecules absorbed into blood
Enzymes
Inside small intestine
gut wall
The blood

Just like convicts, food can't pass through walls...

So that's the basics of digestion — food is broken down into tiny molecules which are absorbed into your bloodstream and transported round your body. Waste is egested (NOT excreted) from the anus.

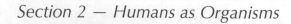

The Skeleton and Muscles

The human skeletal system is made up of 206 bones and the muscular system has around 640 muscles. Together these systems are really important for allowing you to move around.

The **Skeletal System**

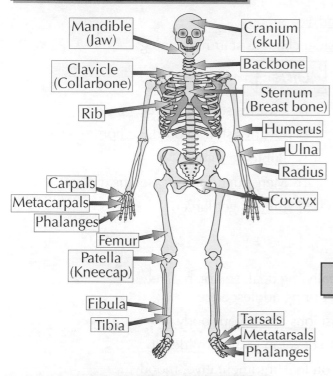

Mandible (Jaw)
Cranium (skull)
Clavicle (Collarbone)
Backbone
Rib
Sternum (Breast bone)
Humerus
Ulna
Radius
Carpals
Metacarpals
Phalanges
Coccyx
Femur
Patella (Kneecap)
Fibula
Tibia
Tarsals
Metatarsals
Phalanges

You need to know about these three functions of the skeletal system:

1) Protection

Bone is rigid and tough so it can protect delicate organs — in particular the brain.

2) Support

1) The skeleton provides a rigid frame for the rest of the body to hang off — kind of like a custom made coat-hanger.

2) All the soft tissues are supported by the skeleton — this allows us to stand up.

3) Movement

1) Muscles are attached to bones (see below).

2) The action of muscles allows the skeleton to move.

3) Joints (e.g. knees and elbows) also allow the skeleton to move. A joint is the place where two bones meet.

The **Muscular System**

1) Muscles are attached to bones via tough bands called tendons.

2) When a muscle contracts it applies a force to the bone it's attached to, which makes the bone move.

3) Muscles are found in pairs round a joint.

Muscle
Tendon
Bone

Antagonistic Muscles Work in Pairs

1) Antagonistic muscles are pairs of muscles that work against each other.

2) One muscle contracts (shortens) while the other one relaxes (lengthens) and vice versa.

3) They are attached to bones with tendons. This allows them to pull on the bone.

4) One muscle can pull the bones towards each other to bend the joint. The other muscle can pull the bones away from each other to straighten the joint.

5) The biceps and triceps muscles in the arm are examples of antagonistic muscles — so when the triceps contracts the biceps returns to its original length and vice versa..

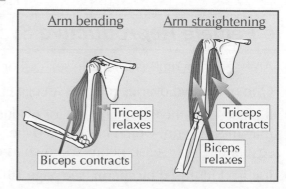

Arm bending
Arm straightening
Triceps relaxes
Triceps contracts
Biceps contracts
Biceps relaxes

A body without bones? Ever seen a tent without poles...

You don't need to learn the names of all those bones — much more important than the names are what the bones and muscles actually do. Make sure you've really sussed how antagonistic muscles work too.

Growing Up

The teenage years — steer well clear, that's my advice. Spots, hormone surges, shape changes, grouchiness, shaving, homework, and to top it all off, ending up with the worst parents IN THE WORLD.

The Nightmare of *Adolescence*

1) <u>Puberty</u> happens when you're between about <u>10 and 18</u>.

2) It's the <u>phase of your life</u> when all these lovely <u>physical changes</u> start happening:

Boys

1) <u>Sex organs</u> get a bit bigger.

2) <u>Testes</u> start to produce <u>sperm</u> and <u>hormones</u>.

3) <u>Pubic hair</u> grows.

4) <u>Hair grows</u> on the face, chest and armpits.

5) <u>Voice deepens</u>.

Girls

1) <u>Ovaries</u> start to release <u>eggs</u>.

2) <u>Ovaries</u> start to produce <u>hormones</u>.

3) <u>Pubic hair</u> grows.

4) <u>Menstruation</u> starts (see next page).

5) <u>Breasts</u> get larger.

Emotional *Changes*

1) Changing from being a child into an adult is a really big deal, so you're likely to go through a whole host of <u>different emotions</u> during adolescence.

2) For example, you may start to feel more <u>self-conscious</u> about your body.

3) You may start wanting more <u>independence</u> and to develop your own <u>identity</u>.

4) Dealing with new feelings like these can make you feel <u>argumentative</u>, <u>moody</u>, <u>frustrated</u> and <u>irritable</u> at times. (Don't worry, these feelings don't last forever.)

The *Male Reproductive* System

1) <u>Sperm</u> are the male <u>sex cells</u> or 'gametes'.

2) Sperm are made in the <u>testes</u> after puberty.

3) Sperm mix with <u>a liquid</u> to make <u>semen</u>, which is <u>ejaculated</u> from the penis during sexual intercourse.

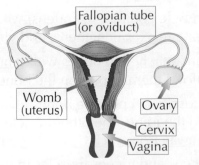

Glands | Tube from bladder
Urethra | Sperm duct
Head of penis | Erectile tissue
Testis | Foreskin (may be removed)
Scrotal sac (scrotum)

The *Female Reproductive* System

1) An <u>egg</u> (or '<u>ovum</u>') is a female <u>sex cell</u> or 'gamete'.

2) <u>One</u> of the two ovaries releases an egg <u>every 28 days</u>.

3) It passes into the <u>fallopian tube</u> (or oviduct) where it may <u>meet sperm</u>, which has entered the vagina during <u>sexual intercourse</u> (sometimes known as copulation).

4) If it <u>isn't fertilised</u> by sperm (see page 18), the egg will <u>die</u> after about a <u>day</u> and pass out of the vagina.

Fallopian tube (or oviduct)
Womb (uterus) | Ovary
Cervix
Vagina

Phew — who'd be a teenager...

I have my suspicions you won't have too much difficulty remembering most of this stuff. Nevertheless, don't miss those easy marks. You might get asked to list the changes that sweep over boys and girls at puberty. If you don't make sure you learn those listed above, you could be throwing away easy marks.

The Menstrual Cycle

Ah-ha, here we have a whole page on a topic adolescent girls might know a fair bit about — the menstrual cycle. It's just the body's way of gearing up to be ready for having a baby.

The **Menstrual Cycle** Takes **28 Days**

1) From the age of puberty females undergo a <u>monthly</u> sequence of events which are collectively known as the <u>menstrual cycle</u>.

2) This involves the body <u>preparing</u> the <u>uterus</u> (womb) in case it receives a <u>fertilised egg</u>.

3) If this doesn't happen, then the egg and uterus lining <u>break down</u> and are <u>lost</u> from the body through the <u>vagina</u> over a period of <u>three</u> to <u>four</u> days, usually.

4) The cycle has <u>four</u> main stages — they are summarised below:

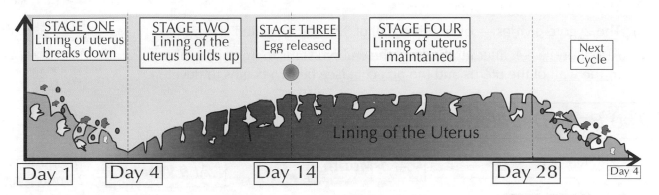

Day 1

<u>Bleeding starts</u> as the <u>lining of the uterus</u> (womb) <u>breaks down</u> and passes out of the vagina — this is what's known as "having a <u>period</u>".

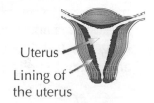

Day 4

The <u>lining</u> of the uterus starts to <u>build up</u> again. It thickens into a spongy layer full of <u>blood vessels</u> ready for <u>implantation</u> (see next page).

Day 14

An <u>egg is released</u> from the ovaries of the female, so this is the <u>most likely</u> time in which a female may become <u>pregnant</u>. (This day may vary from one woman to the next).

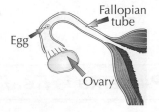

Day 28

The wall remains thick awaiting the <u>arrival</u> of a <u>fertilised egg</u>. If this doesn't happen then this lining <u>breaks down</u>, passes out of the vagina, and the whole cycle <u>starts again</u>.

Menstruation — nothing to do with 'men' whatsoever...

There are quite a few details to learn here. Make sure you know what the four stages of the menstrual cycle are. You also need to know when each stage happens. There's no easy way to learn it I'm afraid — just read it all through, cover the page, see how much you remember, and repeat till you've got it all.

Section 2 — Humans as Organisms

Having a Baby

Adolescence, reproductive systems, the menstrual cycle... they're all needed for having a baby.

Fertilisation Needs to Happen to Make a Baby

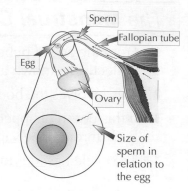

1) During sexual intercourse, millions of sperm are released from the penis into the vagina.

2) The sperm travel to the fallopian tubes where one may fertilise an egg.

3) An egg is fertilised when the nuclei of the sperm and egg cell fuse together. For this to happen the head of a sperm pushes its way through the membrane of the egg cell.

4) When the egg and sperm fuse the parents' genes mix (see p. 29).

5) The fertilised egg is called a zygote.

6) The zygote divides — once it is a ball of 32 cells it's called an embryo.

7) About one week after fertilisation, the embryo starts to implant (embed) in the wall of the uterus and the placenta (see below) begins to develop.

See page 9 for more on the structure and function of egg and sperm cells.

The Baby Develops in the Uterus

Start here ➡

At 39 weeks

The baby is about 520 mm long. It's fully developed and ready to be born.

At 1 Month

The embryo is 6 mm long and has a brain, heart, eyes, ears and legs.

At 9 Weeks

The body is about 25 mm long and is completely formed — it's now called a foetus.

At 3 Months

The foetus is 54 mm long and looks much more like a baby.

At 7 Months

The foetus is 370 mm long and is 'viable'. This means it would have a fair chance of surviving if it were born at this stage.

At 5 Months

It's now about 160 mm long. It kicks and its pesky finger nails can be felt.

The Placenta is Really Important for the Growing Foetus

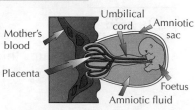

1) The placenta is an organ that's attached to the wall of the uterus.

2) The amniotic sac attaches to the placenta — this sac contains amniotic fluid, which protects the foetus against knocks and bumps.

3) The foetus is attached to the placenta by the umbilical cord.

4) The placenta lets the blood of the foetus and the blood of mother get very close together. This allows the foetus to be nourished (receive the things it needs to grow properly) as oxygen and nutrients pass from the mother to the foetus.

5) It also allows the foetus to eliminate waste products (like carbon dioxide) as they pass from the foetus to the mother.

Gas Exchange

You need to get oxygen from the air into your bloodstream. You also need to get rid of the carbon dioxide that's in your bloodstream. Funnily enough, this exchange of gases happens in your gas exchange system.

You Need to **Breathe** for **Gas Exchange** to Happen

1) The diagram on the right shows some of the structures in the gas exchange system.

2) The process of getting air in and out of the lungs is called breathing. It happens like this:
   - When you breathe in, the diaphragm moves down and the ribs move up. This increases the volume of the chest, which decreases the pressure. So air rushes in to fill the lungs.
   - When you breathe out, the diaphragm moves up and the ribs move down, so air rushes out.

3) When you breathe in, air goes down the trachea, through the bronchi, through the bronchioles and into small air sacs in the lungs called alveoli. These are where gas exchange takes place.

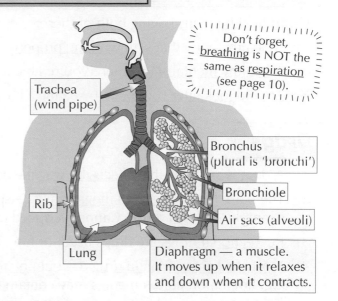

Don't forget, breathing is NOT the same as respiration (see page 10).

Trachea (wind pipe)

Bronchus (plural is 'bronchi')

Bronchiole

Air sacs (alveoli)

Rib

Lung

Diaphragm — a muscle. It moves up when it relaxes and down when it contracts.

Gas Exchange Happens in the Lungs

1) Air is inhaled into the lungs.

2) Some of the oxygen in the inhaled air passes through the walls of the alveoli and into the bloodstream, where it binds to red blood cells.

3) The oxygen is transported by the circulatory system (i.e. the heart, blood vessels and blood) to all body tissues. Cells can then use the oxygen for respiration (see page 10).

4) Carbon dioxide is a waste product of respiration. In the lungs it passes out of the blood and is then breathed out.

5) The lungs are well adapted for gas exchange:

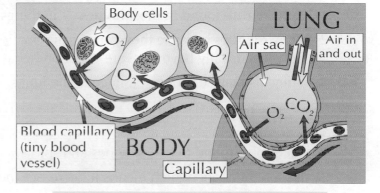

Body cells

CO$_2$

O$_2$

O$_2$

LUNG

Air sac

Air in and out

Blood capillary (tiny blood vessel)

BODY

Capillary

O$_2$ CO$_2$

1) They're moist.
2) They have a good blood supply.
3) The alveoli are folded, which give the lungs a big inside surface area.

Smoking Can Do Lots of Damage

1) Some of the particles in cigarette smoke can irritate the lining of the airways. This can cause inflammation and damage to the lungs.

2) The damage builds up and can eventually lead to a disease called emphysema. This disease destroys alveoli, so it greatly reduces the surface area of the lungs. People with emphysema find it difficult to breathe.

3) And there's more... tar (found in cigarette smoke) contains carcinogens — substances that can cause cancer. Smoking causes cancer of the lung, throat and mouth.

4) Smoking also increases the risk of heart disease — gosh, I think I'll give this smoking thing a miss.

Drugs

Good health is a situation where you're fine and dandy both physically and mentally. Recreational drugs can have serious negative effects on your health.

Health is More Than Just the Absence of Disease

Good health means having both of these:

1) A healthy body that's all working properly with no diseases.

2) A healthy mental state where you're able to cope with the ups and downs of life.

You should look after your body by eating a balanced diet, doing enough exercise and not abusing drugs.

Drugs

1) A drug is anything that affects the way the body works. E.g. it may raise the heart rate or affect vision.

2) There are legal drugs and illegal drugs. Aspirin, caffeine and antibiotics are examples of legal drugs. Cannabis, speed and ecstasy are examples of illegal drugs.

3) Recreational drugs are drugs used for fun. They can be legal or illegal.

4) Most medicines contain drugs — but not all drugs are medicines. E.g. hot lemon cold remedies may contain the drug paracetamol, to reduce the cold symptoms — but tobacco contains the drug nicotine, which is not a medicine.

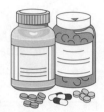

Solvents

1) Solvents are found in most homes — in things like paints, aerosols and glues.

2) They're drugs because they cause hallucinations, which are illusions of the mind. Solvents usually have a severe effect on behaviour and character.

3) They also cause serious damage to the lungs, the brain, liver and kidneys.

Alcohol

1) Alcohol is found in beers, wines and spirits. It's illegal to buy it under the age of 18.

2) It's a depressant, which means it decreases the activity of the brain and slows down responses.

3) It's a poison which affects the brain and liver leading to various health problems, e.g. cirrhosis (liver disease).

4) It impairs judgement which can lead to accidents. It's also very addictive.

Illegal Drugs — Dangerous, Addictive and Life-Wrecking

1) Ecstasy and LSD are hallucinogens. Ecstasy can give the feeling of boundless energy which can lead to overheating, dehydration and sometimes death.

2) Amphetamine (speed) and Methedrine are stimulants. They give a feeling of boundless energy. However, users quickly become psychologically dependent on the drug (i.e. they think they need them), so behaviour and character deteriorate.

3) Barbiturates are depressants. They can help with sleep problems but they're very addictive.

Drugs aren't harmless fun — they're a slippery slope...

There are lots of details here. Make sure you know how drugs such as alcohol, solvents and illegal drugs can affect health. And above all else, make sure you realise the dangers of abusing drugs.

Fighting Disease

If microorganisms (e.g. viruses, bacteria) get inside the body they can cause diseases, making you feel ill.

Viruses

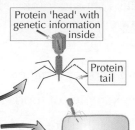

Protein 'head' with genetic information inside

Protein tail

1) Viruses are tiny microorganisms (about 0.00001 mm long).

2) They are strands of genetic information with protein coats.

3) They invade living tissue and take over cells, making them produce millions of copies of themselves.

4) They damage cells and release poisons making you feel ill.

5) Antibiotics don't affect them.

6) Viral diseases include: colds, flu, chickenpox, German measles.

Bacteria

1) Bacteria are larger (about 0.001 mm).

2) They're living cells and are found in most places.

3) They grow and reproduce very rapidly.

4) Some are harmless but others cause disease.

5) They attack body tissue or release poisons, making you ill.

6) Antibiotics do affect them.

7) Bacterial diseases include: tetanus, food poisoning, whooping cough.

Your Body Can Defend Itself Against Disease

1) Your immune system tries to defend your body against disease if microorganisms get into your body.

2) The most important part of your immune system is your white blood cells.

3) These travel round in your blood and attack any microorganisms they come across. They do this in these three ways:

- They eat (engulf) microorganisms.

- They neutralise the poisons produced by microorganisms.

- They make antibodies. Every microorganism has unique molecules on its surface called antigens. White blood cells produce antibodies which lock onto the antigens and kill the microorganisms.

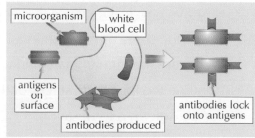

microorganism

white blood cell

antigens on surface

antibodies produced

antibodies lock onto antigens

There Are Other Ways We Can Defend Against Disease...

Vaccinations

1) Vaccinations are a type of 'medicine' that help to defend against disease.

2) Vaccinations usually involve being injected with inactive or dead microorganisms.

3) This causes antibodies to be made by the body, ready for if a real infection happens.

Keeping Things Clean

The best way to defend against disease is to prevent the microorganisms from entering our bodies in the first place. Keeping things clean is a really good way of doing this. For example:

- Encouraging people to wash their hands often (to wash off the microorganisms that cling to our skin when we touch things). This is really important at home and also in public areas to stop microorganisms being passed on to other people.

- Having laws to ensure that places where food is made or prepared are kept clean — this helps to prevent harmful microorganisms getting into the food we eat.

Summary Questions

Well, there's certainly some interesting stuff in Section 2 — all you ever wanted to know about human beings, and a good deal more besides I should think. Now what you've got to do is make sure you learn it all. And here again for your enjoyment I have prepared some more of those splendid questions. All they do is test the basic simple facts. Let's see how much you've learnt so far...

1) Name all five nutrients in a balanced diet and say what each nutrient is important for in the body.

2) For each of the five nutrients, give three examples of foods that contain them.

3) Apart from the five nutrients, give two things that are needed in a balanced diet.

4) What health problem can be caused by: a) a lack of vitamin C?   b) getting too little calcium?

5) Why is it not a good idea to have too much animal fat in your diet?

6) Give three reasons why exercise is important for staying healthy.

7) What is digestion?

8) How does the pancreas help with digestion?

9) What are villi? What is their function (job)?

10) What happens to the waste products of digestion?

11) Why do food molecules need to be broken down before they can be used by the body?

12) Give three functions of the skeleton.

13) What are antagonistic muscles?

14) Explain in terms of 'muscle contraction' how you can move your arm up and down.

15) List five physical changes that occur during adolescence for: a) boys,   b) girls.

16) Describe some of the emotional changes an adolescent may go through.

17) What are the human male and female sex cells called? Where are each of them made?

18) Outline the four main stages of the menstrual cycle and say when they happen.

19) What exactly is fertilisation?

20) What is a zygote?

21) Describe what a human embryo is like at: 9 weeks, 5 months, 7 months.

22) Explain why the placenta is important to a growing foetus.

23) Explain how we breathe air in and out.

24) What gases are exchanged in the lungs when we inhale? Where does each gas move from and to?

25) Give three ways in which the lungs are well-adapted for gas exchange.

26) Give three diseases that can be caused by smoking.

27) What is a 'drug'?

28) Give two negative health effects that can be caused by: a) solvents,   b) alcohol.

29) Name three illegal drugs.

30) Name one disease caused by: a) a virus,   b) bacteria.

31) List the three ways that white blood cells fight microorganisms.

32) How do vaccinations help to defend against disease?

33) Why is it important that people wash their hands often?

Section 2 — Humans as Organisms

Plant Reproduction

Plants, like all living things, need to reproduce. And that's where a plant's pretty flowers come in...

The Flower Contains the Reproductive Organs

1) In flowering plants, reproduction starts with <u>pollination</u> — this is where <u>pollen grains</u> are transferred from a <u>stamen</u> (a <u>male</u> part of a flower) to a <u>stigma</u> (a <u>female</u> part of a flower).

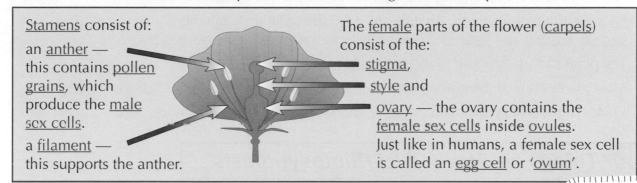

Stamens consist of:

an <u>anther</u> — this contains <u>pollen grains</u>, which produce the <u>male sex cells</u>.

a <u>filament</u> — this supports the anther.

The <u>female</u> parts of the flower (<u>carpels</u>) consist of the:

<u>stigma</u>,

<u>style</u> and

<u>ovary</u> — the ovary contains the <u>female sex cells</u> inside <u>ovules</u>. Just like in humans, a female sex cell is called an <u>egg cell</u> or '<u>ovum</u>'.

2) Pollination often happens with help from <u>insects</u> or the <u>wind</u>.

Gamete is another word for a sex cell.

Fertilisation is the Joining of Sex Cells

After <u>pollination</u>, the next step in plant reproduction is <u>fertilisation</u>. Here's how it works...

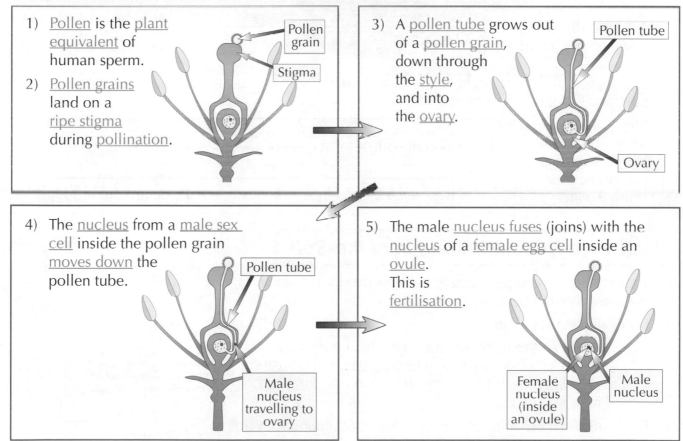

1) <u>Pollen</u> is the <u>plant equivalent</u> of human sperm.

2) <u>Pollen grains</u> land on a <u>ripe stigma</u> during <u>pollination</u>.

Pollen grain

Stigma

3) A <u>pollen tube</u> grows out of a <u>pollen grain</u>, down through the <u>style</u>, and into the <u>ovary</u>.

Pollen tube

Ovary

4) The <u>nucleus</u> from a <u>male sex cell</u> inside the pollen grain <u>moves down</u> the pollen tube.

Pollen tube

Male nucleus travelling to ovary

5) The male <u>nucleus fuses</u> (joins) with the <u>nucleus</u> of a <u>female egg cell</u> inside an <u>ovule</u>. This is <u>fertilisation</u>.

Female nucleus (inside an ovule)

Male nucleus

After <u>fertilisation</u> the <u>ovule</u> develops into a <u>seed</u>, which can eventually grow into a <u>new plant</u>.

Now that's what I call flower power...

Who'd have thought all that goes on inside a flower. Make sure you understand what happens during fertilisation — a nucleus from a male sex cell joins up with one from a female sex cell.

Plant Nutrition

Think about this: plants make their own food — it's a nice trick if you can do it.

Photosynthesis: Making Food Using Sunlight

1) Photosynthesis is a <u>chemical process</u> which takes place in <u>every green plant</u>.

2) Photosynthesis basically produces <u>food</u> — in the form of <u>glucose</u>.

3) <u>Glucose</u> is a <u>carbohydrate</u>. That means it's made up of the elements <u>carbon</u>, <u>oxygen</u> and <u>hydrogen</u> (see page 43 for more about elements).

4) The plant can use glucose to <u>increase its biomass</u> — i.e. to <u>grow</u>.

5) Most plants convert the glucose into <u>starch</u>, which is easier to <u>store</u>.

6) Photosynthesis happens in all the <u>green bits</u> of a plant but <u>mainly in the leaves</u>.

Four Things are Needed for Photosynthesis...

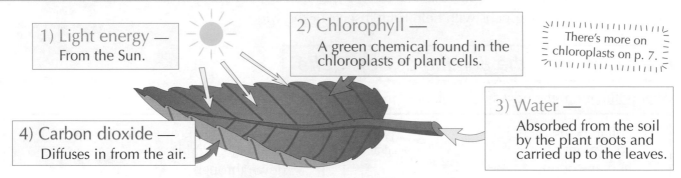

1) Light energy — From the Sun.

2) Chlorophyll — A green chemical found in the chloroplasts of plant cells.

There's more on chloroplasts on p. 7.

3) Water — Absorbed from the soil by the plant roots and carried up to the leaves.

4) Carbon dioxide — Diffuses in from the air.

1) <u>Chlorophyll</u> absorbs <u>sunlight</u> and uses its energy to convert <u>carbon dioxide</u> and <u>water</u> into <u>glucose</u>. <u>Oxygen</u> is also produced.

2) This <u>word equation</u> summarises what happens during photosynthesis. Learn it well.

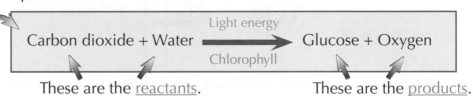

$$\text{Carbon dioxide} + \text{Water} \xrightarrow[\text{Chlorophyll}]{\text{Light energy}} \text{Glucose} + \text{Oxygen}$$

These are the <u>reactants</u>.　These are the <u>products</u>.

Plants Also Need Minerals from the Soil

1) To <u>keep healthy</u> and <u>grow properly</u> plants need some elements that they get from <u>minerals</u> in the <u>soil</u>.

2) For example, they need:
   - <u>nitrates</u> — these provide <u>nitrogen</u> which is needed for making <u>proteins</u> (used in <u>tissue repair</u> and <u>growth</u>).
   - <u>magnesium</u> — this is an important part of <u>chlorophyll</u>. Plants <u>couldn't photosynthesise</u> without it.

3) Plants absorb these minerals through their <u>roots</u> (along with <u>water</u>).

4) <u>Root hair cells</u> are specialised so they are good at <u>absorption</u> (see page 9).

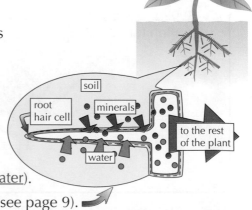

soil

root hair cell

minerals

to the rest of the plant

water

Hmm, it's all clever stuff — just make sure you learn it...

Remember, plants don't get food from the soil — they make it themselves using photosynthesis. They do get water and some of the elements they need to grow properly from the soil though.

Photosynthesis Experiments

You can't tell photosynthesis is happening by looking at a plant — you need to do an experiment or two...

You Can *Investigate Photosynthesis* by *Collecting Gas*

This is a simple experiment which shows that photosynthesis is going on:

1) Get a sample of a water plant such as *Elodea*.

2) Put it under a <u>funnel</u> in a beaker of <u>sodium hydrogen-carbonate solution</u> — this provides carbon dioxide and water. Put a <u>measuring cylinder</u> over the top.

3) The *Elodea* will produce bubbles of <u>oxygen</u> as it photosynthesises.

4) Use the measuring cylinder to <u>measure</u> the amount of <u>oxygen produced</u> in a <u>given time</u> — this will show how <u>fast</u> photosynthesis is happening. (Or you could just <u>count the bubbles</u>.)

5) You can check that the gas you've collected is oxygen by seeing if it will <u>relight a glowing splint</u> (see p. 57).

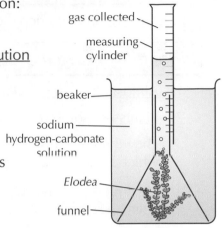

gas collected

measuring cylinder

beaker

sodium hydrogen-carbonate solution

Elodea

funnel

You could use this experiment to investigate how <u>different factors</u> affect the rate of photosynthesis, e.g. by changing the <u>amount of light</u> the plant has and <u>repeating</u> the experiment.

The Almost Legendary *Starch Test*

You can show that <u>light</u> is needed for <u>starch production</u> with this experiment:

Remember, plants produce starch following photosynthesis (see p. 24).

 ①

 ②

 ③

Put a plant in darkness for 24 hours to get rid of all the starch from all the leaves.

Put a strip of black tape on one of the leaves. Leave the plant in light for 24 hours.

Remove the black tape and remove the leaf from the plant. Boil the leaf in water for a few minutes to soften it.

 ④

 ⑤

 ⑥

Make sure you're working safely (see p. 4) — keep the ethanol away from the Bunsen burner.

Put the leaf in a boiling tube and cover it with ethanol. Put the boiling tube in hot water so the ethanol boils. This will remove the green colour (chlorophyll) from the leaf.

Dip the leaf in water to wash it.

Now do the iodine test for starch. Drip brown iodine solution all over the leaf. The iodine will turn blue-black in places where starch is present.

The results:

1) Iodine goes <u>blue-black</u> in parts that have been <u>photosynthesising</u> (where there's <u>starch</u>).

2) If the iodine stays <u>brown</u> then there's <u>no starch</u> present — which means that those parts of the plant were <u>not</u> photosynthesising.

3) The bit of the leaf that was covered in <u>black tape</u> didn't get any light, so that bit <u>didn't photosynthesise</u>. So it didn't make any starch – which is why the iodine <u>stayed brown</u>.

The Importance of Plants

Plants live a quiet life — they just sit there soaking up the sun and swaying in the breeze, not a care in the world... But simple as they are, they're super-important for life on Earth...

Almost *All Living Things Depend* on *Plants*

Almost all life on Earth depends on plants. Without them, we just wouldn't be here. Here's why...

Plants *Capture* the *Sun's Energy*

1) Almost all energy on Earth comes from the Sun.

2) Plants use some of the Sun's energy to make food (glucose) during photosynthesis (see page 24).

3) They then use this food to build "organic molecules" (things like carbohydrates and proteins), which become part of the plants' cells. These organic molecules store the Sun's energy.

4) The energy gets passed on from plants to animals when animals eat the plants. It gets passed on again when these animals are eaten by other animals.

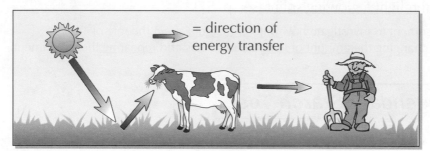

= direction of energy transfer

Without plants, we wouldn't have any food to eat.

5) Only plants, algae (seaweeds) and some bacteria are able to carry out photosynthesis. So nearly all living things rely on plants to capture and store the Sun's energy.

Plants *Release Oxygen* and *Take in Carbon Dioxide*

1) All living things respire (see page 10).

2) When plants and animals carry out aerobic respiration, they take in oxygen (O_2) from the atmosphere and release carbon dioxide (CO_2).

3) When plants photosynthesise, they do the opposite — they release oxygen and take in carbon dioxide.

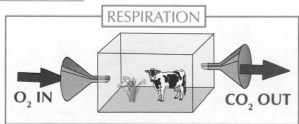

RESPIRATION

O_2 IN CO_2 OUT

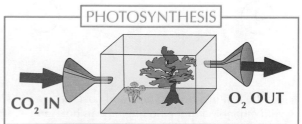

PHOTOSYNTHESIS

CO_2 IN O_2 OUT

4) So photosynthesis helps make sure there's always plenty of oxygen around for respiration. It also helps to stop the carbon dioxide level in the atmosphere from getting too high (see next page).

Make sure this stuff is imPLANTed firmly into your brain...

If there's one thing you should get from this page it's this — plants are really, really important. Even if you live on a nothing-but-meat diet you still rely on plants for your food (without plants those tasty cows wouldn't even exist). And plants help to control the balance of gases in the atmosphere too.

The Carbon Cycle

Carbon is really important — it's a part of all living things. It's pretty lucky then that we won't run out of carbon, because it's constantly being recycled in a process called... wait for it... the carbon cycle.

This Diagram Shows the **Carbon Cycle**...

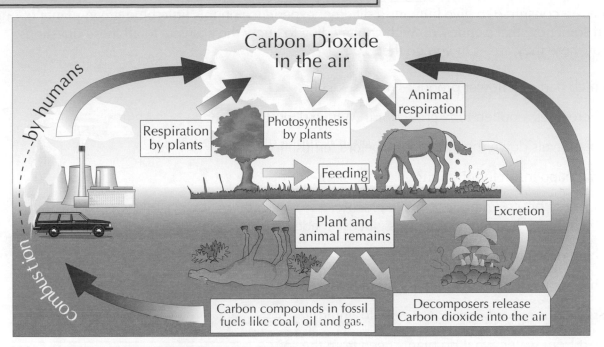

Carbon is constantly being <u>cycled</u> — from the <u>air</u>, through <u>food chains</u> and eventually back out into the <u>air</u> again. Make sure you learn these points:

1) **Photosynthesis** Removes **Carbon Dioxide** from the **Air**

1) <u>Green plants</u> take in <u>carbon dioxide</u> from the air during <u>photosynthesis</u> (see page 24).

2) The plants use the carbon to make <u>carbohydrates</u>, <u>fats</u> and <u>proteins</u>.

2) **Carbon** is **Passed Along** the **Food Chain** When Animals **Feed**

1) Some of the carbon in plants is <u>passed on</u> to <u>animals</u> when they <u>eat</u> the plants.

2) The animals then use the carbon to make <u>fats</u> and <u>proteins</u> of their own.
The carbon moves along the <u>food chain</u> when the animals are eaten by other animals.

3) **Respiration** and **Combustion** Return **Carbon Dioxide** to the **Air**

1) Some carbon is <u>returned</u> to the <u>air</u> as <u>carbon dioxide</u> when plants and animals <u>respire</u> (see p. 10).

2) When plants and animals <u>die</u>, <u>decomposers</u> (like bacteria and fungi) <u>feed</u> on them. Decomposers also feed on <u>animal waste</u>. When the decomposers <u>respire</u>, carbon dioxide is returned to the air.

3) Some <u>dead plant and animal remains</u> get buried and eventually form <u>fossil fuels</u>.
When fossil fuels are <u>burnt</u> (<u>combustion</u>) this releases <u>carbon dioxide</u> back into the <u>air</u>.

All this cycling's tiring me out...

An important thing to remember about the carbon cycle is that there's only one process that takes carbon out of the atmosphere — photosynthesis. Respiration and combustion both put it back.

Section 3 — Plants as Organisms

Summary Questions

Green plants are great aren't they? What I really like about them is that they're all so clean and fresh — human and animal biology always seems to end up so gory with all sorts of gruesome diagrams and horrid diseases. But plants have such simple lives. They just seem to "go with the flow", with no worries — and let's face it, that's a nice trick if you can do it.

Alas nature conspired to give humans a different experience on this little blue-green planet of ours — and somehow that's ended up with you needing to know the answers to all these questions. Anyway, here they are. Off you go then...

1) Which part of a flower produces male sex cells?

2) Where does a pollen tube grow from? Where does it grow to?

3) What travels down the pollen tube before fertilisation?

4) What happens in fertilisation?

5) Plants use photosynthesis to make glucose.
    Which three chemical elements is glucose made up from?

6) What do plants store glucose as?

7) What are the four things needed for photosynthesis to happen?

8) Write out the word equation for photosynthesis.

9) Apart from water, what do plants need from the soil?

10) Why does a plant need nitrates?

11) Why does a plant need magnesium?

12) Why are root hair cells so important to plants?

13) Describe how you could investigate whether a water plant photosynthesises
    more quickly in dim light or bright light.

14) Jamie does an experiment to test for the presence of starch in a leaf.
    a) During his experiment he soaks the leaf in boiling ethanol. Why does he do this?
    b) What chemical should Jamie use to test for the presence of starch in the leaf?
       Describe what would happen if there was starch present.

15) Explain why most living things rely on plants for energy.

16) Apart from providing us with energy, explain why it is important to other living things
    that plants carry out photosynthesis.

17) Which process in the carbon cycle removes carbon dioxide from the air?

18) In the carbon cycle, describe how carbon gets from the air into your body.

19) Carbon from the carbon dioxide in the air can become part of plant tissues through
    photosynthesis. It can then become part of animal tissues through feeding.
    Name four ways that this carbon can find its way back into the air.

DNA and Inheritance

DNA's brilliant stuff — it's like your body's own instruction manual. When you're being made, you get bits of DNA from your mum and bits from your dad — this is how you inherit characteristics.

Chromosomes, DNA and Genes

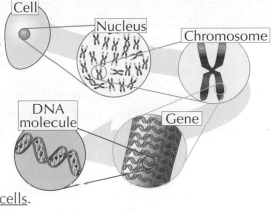

1) Most cells in your body have a <u>nucleus</u>. The nucleus contains <u>chromosomes</u>.

2) Chromosomes are <u>long, coiled up lengths</u> of a molecule called <u>DNA</u>.

3) DNA is a long <u>list</u> of <u>chemical instructions</u> on how to build an organism.

4) A <u>gene</u> is a <u>short section</u> of a chromosome (and so a short section of <u>DNA</u>).

5) Genes control the <u>production</u> of different <u>proteins</u> within <u>cells</u>.

6) Genes <u>determine</u> many of our <u>characteristics</u>, e.g. hair colour, eye colour, hairiness, etc. Different genes control <u>different</u> characteristics.

We Inherit Characteristics from Our Parents

1) <u>Sperm</u> and <u>egg cells</u> (ova) each have a <u>nucleus</u>. Just like other cells, the nucleus contains <u>genes</u>.

2) During <u>fertilisation</u>, the nuclei of a sperm and an egg cell <u>fuse</u> together, producing a <u>zygote</u> (see page 18).

3) When this happens, genes from the <u>mother</u> and <u>father</u> get <u>mixed together</u>. The zygote gets <u>half</u> of its genes from its father and <u>half</u> from its mother.

4) Since genes control <u>characteristics</u>, the <u>zygote</u> develops into a baby with a <u>mixture</u> of its <u>parents' characteristics</u>. This is how you 'inherit' your parents' characteristics.

Dad has gene for big ears.

Son gets half of his genes from his dad — he has inherited the gene for big ears.

Selective Breeding is Very Simple

1) All this knowledge about <u>offspring</u> (babies) <u>inheriting characteristics</u> from their parents is put to good use in <u>selective breeding</u>.

2) Selective breeding is where humans try to develop <u>particular varieties</u> of plants or animals with <u>desirable characteristics</u>.

3) For example, <u>dogs</u> are selectively bred to have desirable characteristics such as a particular <u>size</u>, <u>appearance</u> or <u>behaviour</u>.

4) This example shows how a dog breeder could use selective breeding to get a <u>very large</u> dog:

> 1) Select the <u>largest</u> dogs available and <u>breed them together</u>.
>
> 2) Select the <u>largest</u> of the <u>offspring</u> and <u>breed them together</u>.
>
> 3) Continue this process over <u>several generations</u>, and the dogs get <u>larger</u> and <u>larger</u>.

This is the basic process used in all cases of selective breeding (i.e. select the best of your stock, breed them together, repeat the process over many generations).

Genes were OK — it was inheriting undies I never liked...

I can see three main headings, seventeen numbered points and three pictures — learn them all.

Variation

This page is all about differences between organisms — both big, obvious differences, like those between a tree and a cow, and less obvious differences, like people having different blood groups.

Different **Species** Have Different **Genes**

1) All living things in the world are <u>different</u> — we say that they show <u>variation</u>.

2) A human, a cow, a dandelion and a tree all look different because they're different <u>species</u>. These differences <u>between</u> species occur because their <u>genes</u> are very <u>different</u>.

3) But you also see variation <u>within a species</u>, i.e. plants or animals that have <u>basically</u> the <u>same</u> genes will also show differences between them, e.g. skin colour, height, flower size, etc. Any <u>difference</u> is known as a <u>characteristic feature</u>.

4) Characteristic features can be <u>inherited</u> (come from your parents via genes) or they can be <u>environmental</u> (caused by your surroundings).

See the next page for more on inherited and environmental variation.

Continuous and **Discontinuous** Variation

Variation <u>within a species</u> can either be classed as <u>continuous</u> or <u>discontinuous</u>.

Continuous Variation — *the feature can vary over a* **range of values**

1) Examples of this are things like <u>height</u>, <u>weight</u>, <u>skin colour</u>, <u>intelligence</u>, <u>leaf area</u>, etc. where the feature can have <u>any value at all</u> — within a certain <u>range</u>. If you did a survey of kids' heights you could plot the results on a chart like the one opposite (the heights would be collected into groups to give the bars).

2) The smooth <u>distribution curve</u> drawn on afterwards (the red line) shows much better the <u>continuous</u> way that values for height actually vary.

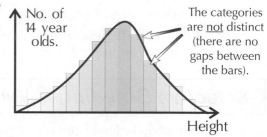

No. of 14 year olds.

The categories are <u>not</u> distinct (there are no gaps between the bars).

Height

Discontinuous Variation — *the feature can only take* **certain values**

1) An example of this is a person's <u>blood group</u>, where there are just <u>four distinct options</u>, <u>NOT</u> a whole <u>continuous range</u>.

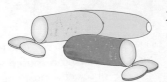

2) Another example is the <u>colour of a courgette</u>. A courgette is either yellow, light green or dark green — there's <u>no range</u> of values.

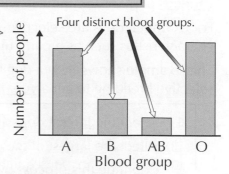

Number of people

Four distinct blood groups.

A   B   AB   O
Blood group

Variationvariationvariation — **guess what type of variation that is...**

Don't let the fancy word "variation" put you off. People seem to think it must mean something really complicated. It just means "differences" (between any living things). You can have variation (differences) between different species, and you can have variation (differences) within one species too.

Inherited and Environmental Variation

Variation between organisms can be caused by their genes, or by different things in their environment.

Inherited and Environmental Variation in Animals

1) We inherit <u>genes</u> from our parents, and with them come a <u>combination</u> of both our parents' characteristics. This is <u>inherited variation</u>.

2) <u>Environmental variation</u> is all to do with the effect of "<u>upbringing</u>". People sometimes say "we're all a product of our environment" — which just means that our <u>abilities</u> and the way we <u>look</u> and <u>behave</u> depend, at least <u>partly</u>, on our <u>upbringing</u>.

3) <u>Identical twins</u> both inherit exactly the <u>same genes</u>, and obviously these control most of their characteristics.

4) However one twin could, say, become much <u>heavier</u> if they <u>ate a lot more</u>. This would be a case of <u>environmental variation</u>.

Few Animal Characteristics are Totally Unaffected by Environment

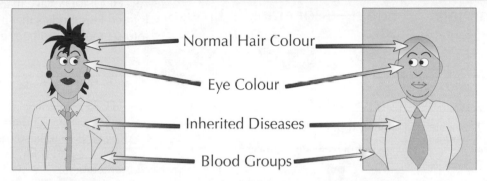

Normal Hair Colour

Eye Colour

Inherited Diseases

Blood Groups

1) The <u>four characteristics</u> shown above are pretty much the <u>only</u> ones which are <u>not affected</u> at all by <u>environment</u> (i.e. upbringing).

2) <u>Most other</u> characteristics of <u>animals</u> are affected by a mixture of <u>genetic</u> and <u>environmental</u> factors — e.g. <u>weight</u>, <u>skin colour</u>, <u>intelligence</u>, <u>athletic ability</u>, etc.

Inherited and Environmental Variation in Plants

1) <u>Plants</u> inherit characteristics through their <u>genes</u> just like <u>animals</u> do.

2) Plants are also affected by their <u>environment</u>. In particular, plants are affected <u>a lot</u> by these <u>four important factors</u>:

❶ Temperature ❷ Sunlight
❸ Moisture ❹ Soil conditions

3) Just a little more <u>light</u> or <u>warmth</u> or <u>water</u> may <u>double</u> the size of a plant — whereas any <u>animal</u> would be <u>barely affected</u> by the same changes in environment.

Don't like the colour of your eyes? Blame your parents...

Pretty straightforward this page — remember that some characteristics are only controlled by genes, and the rest are controlled by a mix of genes and environmental factors. Easy-peasy, satsuma-squeezy.

Classification

It seems to be a basic human urge to want to classify things — that's the case in biology anyway...

All Living Things Can Be Classified Into Groups

1) The similarities and differences between organisms allow us to classify them into taxonomic groups.

2) Living things are first divided into five kingdoms:
   - Plants are fixed in the ground, so they can't move around. They make their own food (see p. 24).
   - Animals move about the place and they can't make their own food.
   - Fungi can't move around, but they don't make their own food (so they're not the same as plants).
   - Monerans are single-celled organisms that do not have a nucleus — e.g. bacteria.
   - Protists are also single-celled organisms, but they do have a nucleus — e.g. amoeba.

3) The kingdoms are then subdivided into smaller and smaller groups as the diagram below shows...

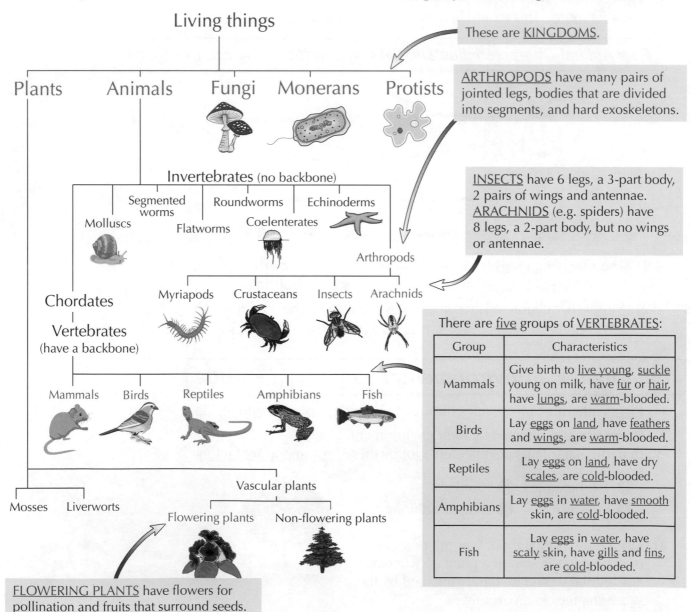

These are KINGDOMS.

ARTHROPODS have many pairs of jointed legs, bodies that are divided into segments, and hard exoskeletons.

INSECTS have 6 legs, a 3-part body, 2 pairs of wings and antennae. ARACHNIDS (e.g. spiders) have 8 legs, a 2-part body, but no wings or antennae.

There are five groups of VERTEBRATES:

Group	Characteristics
Mammals	Give birth to live young, suckle young on milk, have fur or hair, have lungs, are warm-blooded.
Birds	Lay eggs on land, have feathers and wings, are warm-blooded.
Reptiles	Lay eggs on land, have dry scales, are cold-blooded.
Amphibians	Lay eggs in water, have smooth skin, are cold-blooded.
Fish	Lay eggs in water, have scaly skin, have gills and fins, are cold-blooded.

FLOWERING PLANTS have flowers for pollination and fruits that surround seeds.

Taxonomic groups — they're in a class of their own...

That diagram looks pretty scary! Thankfully you don't need to know it all in detail. Make sure you learn everything in the numbered list at the top of the page and in the purple boxes and you'll be fine.

Section 4 — Inheritance, Variation and Classification

Using Keys

Step 1: place key in lock. Step 2: turn key anticlockw — oh wait, wrong type of key...

Keys are Used to Identify a Specimen's Group

1) You could use a key to identify which group a specimen belongs to.

In this case, a specimen is an individual organism that is thought to be typical of all the individuals in its group.

2) A key involves a series of questions which all have two possible answers.

3) The two answers divide a group into two parts.

4) Further questions continue to divide the group up until you are just left with one group that your specimen belongs to.

The Key is to Follow the Method

1) Take a good look at your specimen and start with Question 1.

2) Follow the instructions on each question for whichever answer is true. Carry on answering the questions until you're able to name the group your specimen belongs to.

Try Working Through This Key

Choose one of the insects below, then see if you can follow the key to correctly identify it.

You need to be able to recognise the abdomen (the bit with the tail — on the left of the insects below) the head (on the right of the insects below), and the thorax (which is the bit with the legs attached).

 A   B   C   D   E

1) Is its head smaller than the thorax?	YES — go to question 2	NO — go to question 4
2) Does it have a forked tail?	YES — go to question 3	NO — then it's a thrip.
3) Is the abdomen long and thin?	YES — then it's a web spinner	NO — then it's a sucking louse.
4) Is the head rounded?	YES — then it's a termite.	NO — then it's a bird louse.

Answers — A = webspinner, B = sucking louse, C = thrip, D = termite, E = bird louse.

Don't let all these keys bug you too much...

Keys are dead simple. But be careful with them — many people mess up easy questions in their exam because they don't concentrate quite hard enough on picky details. You have been warned...

Section 4 — Inheritance, Variation and Classification

Summary Questions

Section 4 is fairly basic stuff really, but there are one or two fancy words which might cause you quite a bit of grief until you've made the effort to learn exactly what they mean: "DNA" is just a list of instructions for how any living organism is put together; "variation" just means "differences", etc., etc. These questions aren't the easiest you could find, but they test exactly what you know and find out exactly what you don't. You need to be able to answer them all, because all they do is test the basic facts. You must practise these questions over and over again until you can just sail through them.

1) Where do you find chromosomes?

2) What are chromosomes made of?

3) What is a gene? What do genes control?

4) Which parts of a sperm and an egg cell fuse together during fertilisation?

5) What proportion of genes in a zygote comes from the mother?

6) Explain why you inherit characteristics from both of your parents.

7) Explain how selective breeding can lead to new varieties of plant or animal.

8) What does variation mean?

9) Why do different species look different?

10) What is a characteristic feature?

11) What is continuous variation? Give three examples.

12) What is discontinuous variation? Give two examples.

13) Give one way in which a graph showing continuous variation would differ from a graph showing discontinuous variation.

14) What is inherited variation?

15) What is environmental variation?

16) Give four characteristics of animals which are totally unaffected by the environment.

17) Give four characteristics of animals which are influenced by genes and the environment.

18) List four environmental factors which could affect how well a plant grows.

19) We can classify all living things into one of five groups. What do we call these groups? List them.

20) How are fungi different to plants?

21) How are monerans different to protists?

22) What is the difference between a vertebrate animal and an invertebrate animal?

23) Give three features of an arthropod.

24) How do insects differ from arachnids? Give three ways.

25) List the five groups of vertebrates, and give three characteristics for each group.

26) Give two features of flowering plants.

27) Describe how you could use a key to identify which group a specimen belongs to.

Section 4 — Inheritance, Variation and Classification

Interdependence and Food Webs

It probably won't surprise you to learn that organisms depend on other organisms for their survival.

Organisms in a Habitat are Interdependent

1) The <u>place</u> where an organism lives is called its <u>habitat</u>, e.g. a freshwater pond or a hedgerow.

2) Many <u>different organisms</u> can live in the <u>same</u> habitat. E.g. look at this <u>freshwater pond</u> habitat:

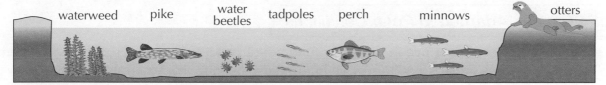

waterweed   pike   water beetles   tadpoles   perch   minnows   otters

3) The <u>organisms</u> in a habitat are <u>interdependent</u> — they <u>need each other</u> to survive.

Food Webs are Made of Lots of Food Chains

1) <u>Food chains</u> show <u>what</u> is <u>eaten</u> by <u>what</u>. For example:

waterweed   → Food for →   minnow   → Food for →   pike   → Food for →   otter

2) Food webs contain <u>many</u> interlinked <u>food chains</u>, like this:

Otter
Pike
Water beetle
Tadpole
Perch
Minnow
Waterweed

<u>Top carnivore</u>
— an animal that is not eaten by anything else.
<u>Tertiary consumer</u>
— an animal that eats secondary consumers.
<u>Secondary consumer</u>
— an animal that eats primary consumers.
<u>Primary consumer</u>
— an animal that eats <u>producers</u> (plants).
<u>Producer</u> — all <u>plants</u> are <u>producers</u>.
They use the Sun's energy to make their own food.

3) The organisms in a food web are all <u>interdependent</u> — a <u>change</u> in <u>one organism</u> can <u>affect others</u>.

> E.g. — What happens if the minnows all die?

1) The <u>tadpoles</u> may be <u>less</u> likely to get eaten as there are no minnows there to eat them.

2) <u>Water beetles</u> may be <u>less</u> likely to get eaten (by perch who'll get hungry without minnows).

3) The <u>waterweeds</u> may be <u>more</u> likely to get eaten (since the numbers of tadpoles will increase).

Poisons Build Up as They are Passed Along a Food Chain

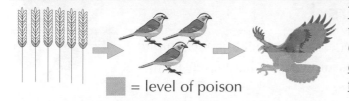

■ = level of poison

<u>Toxic materials</u> (poisons) can sometimes get into food chains and <u>harm</u> the organisms involved. Organisms <u>higher up</u> the food chain (usually the <u>top carnivores</u>) are likely to be the <u>worst affected</u> as the <u>toxins accumulate</u> (build up) as they are passed along.

Learn about food webs — but don't get tangled up...

Once you've learnt everything on this page, practise this typical food web question: "If the number of otters decreased, give one reason why the number of water beetles might a) decrease   b) increase".*

Adaptations

Adaptations are the features that organisms have that make them better suited to their environment.

Plants and Animals Adapt to Their Environment

1) The conditions in an organism's habitat make up its environment, e.g. how hot it is, amount of water.

2) Plants and animals develop features and become adapted to their environments over millions of years.

Arctic Hare — Adapted to Polar Conditions

Arctic hares live in the Arctic tundra — a very cold, icy and rocky environment. They are adapted to survive in this harsh habitat. For example, they have:

- A thick coat of fur to keep body heat in.
- Short ears and a round body shape, which gives the minimum possible surface area to reduce heat loss from the skin.
- A coat that is a similar colour to their surroundings, so they blend in.

Cactus — Adapted to Desert Conditions

Cacti live in deserts that are very hot and dry. They have adapted to live in this habitat by having:

- Spines instead of leaves — to reduce water loss.
- A thick stem for storing water in.
- Shallow but extensive roots to ensure water is absorbed quickly over a large area.

Adapting to Daily Changes

Daily changes in conditions like light, temperature or moisture levels in the air affect the behaviour of plants and animals. They adapt to deal with these daily changes — for example:

1) Arctic hares are generally nocturnal, which helps them avoid predators that hunt during the day.

2) A cactus has small pores (holes) in its surface, which water vapour can escape from. These pores close during the day to reduce water loss.

Adapting to Seasonal Changes

Most organisms have to adapt to seasonal changes in temperature, light, availability of water and food, e.g:

1) Arctic hares have a white coat during winter, which acts as camouflage against the snow. In summer, when the snow melts, their fur turns brownish-grey to blend in with the ground.

2) Cacti only grow flowers during the rainy season. During long dry periods the flowers drop off to conserve water.

Measuring Different Physical Factors

You can measure a variety of physical factors in an organism's habitat. For example:

1) Light intensity (brightness of the light) can be measured with a light intensity meter.

2) Temperature can be measured with a thermometer.

Grey hares — they must be getting old...

Make sure you understand what adaptations are and why they're important. You need to know about the habitat of at least one animal and one plant and how the organism adapts to daily and seasonal changes.

Population Size

A "population" is how many of one particular type of plant or animal there is in a particular place.

Population Size is Affected by Competition...

1) Organisms need certain <u>resources</u> in order to survive, e.g. <u>food</u>, <u>water</u>, <u>space</u>, <u>light</u> and <u>mates</u>. These resources are often <u>limited</u> in a habitat.

2) Organisms that are the <u>best at competing</u> for these resources are <u>more likely</u> to <u>survive</u> and <u>reproduce</u>, so their population size may <u>grow</u>.

3) For example, some <u>bacteria</u> produce <u>antibiotics</u> — these <u>kill other species</u> of bacteria in the same area. This means the <u>population size</u> of the <u>antibiotic-producing bacteria</u> is likely to <u>grow</u>, as there's <u>less competition</u> from other species of bacteria for food and space.

4) <u>Plants</u> need to compete with each other for <u>sunlight</u>, so they can <u>photosynthesise</u>. In an area where there are <u>lots of plants</u> (such as a <u>rainforest</u>), species of plants that can <u>grow tallest</u> are likely to have a <u>greater population size</u> than shorter species, as they get <u>more light</u>.

... and Predation

1) <u>Predation</u> is where an organism (the <u>predator</u>) kills and eats another organism (the <u>prey</u>).

2) If the population size of a <u>predator</u> in a habitat increases, <u>more prey</u> will be eaten so the population size of the prey will <u>decrease</u>.

3) If the population size of the <u>prey increases</u>, the population size of the <u>predator</u> may also <u>increase</u> as there is <u>more food</u> available.

Use Quadrats to Estimate Population Size

A <u>quadrat</u> is a <u>square</u> frame enclosing a <u>known area</u>, e.g. 1 m². Quadrats are great for estimating the <u>population sizes</u> of <u>small</u>, <u>slow-moving</u> or <u>still</u> organisms — e.g. daisies. To estimate the population size of an organism in <u>one area</u>, just follow these steps:

A quadrat.

1) Place a <u>quadrat</u> on the ground at a <u>random point</u> within the area.

2) <u>Count</u> all the organisms <u>within</u> the quadrat and <u>record</u> the result.

3) <u>Repeat</u> steps 1 and 2 as many times as you can.

4) <u>Work out</u> the <u>mean number of organisms per quadrat</u>.

E.g. Ty counted the number of daisies in 7 quadrats and recorded these results: 18, 20, 22, 23, 23, 23, 25

Here the MEAN is: $\dfrac{\text{TOTAL number of organisms}}{\text{NUMBER of quadrats}} = \dfrac{154}{7} = \underline{22}$ daisies per quadrat.

5) Then work out the <u>mean number of organisms per m²</u>. (If your quadrat has an area of 1 m², this is the <u>same</u> as the mean number of organisms per quadrat, worked out above.)

6) Finally multiply the <u>mean</u> by the <u>total area</u> (in m²) of the habitat.

For example, if the area of an open field is 800 m² and there are 22 daisies per m², then the <u>size of the daisy population</u> is 22 x 800 = <u>17 600</u>.

There's no runner-up prize in the competition for survival...

I'm glad I'm a human — we're great at competing for resources and don't have to worry too much about predation, so our population size is on the up. And we get to use those quadrat thingies.

Protecting Living Things

Humans depend on other organisms to survive — we need to protect them.

Development Has to be Sustainable

1) Humans use resources from the Earth to survive. For example, we use many different animals and plants for things like food, drugs and clothes. Also, we use fossil fuels for energy (see p. 104).

2) As the human population grows, we'll use more of these resources and produce more pollution.

3) If we're not careful, we could end up losing some of our valuable resources and damaging the environment.

4) We need to manage the way we use resources so that the needs of our growing population can be met without harming the environment — this is called sustainable development.

It's Important to Conserve Species and Habitats

1) Human activities can greatly affect the environment and the population size of a species.

2) Sometimes our actions cause the population size of a species to fall directly — e.g. by hunting.

3) Other times our activities affect habitats — e.g. chopping down trees to make way for buildings. This in turn can affect the population size of a species.

- When an organism's habitat is destroyed or changed in some way, the organism may no longer be able to survive and reproduce successfully.
- This could mean its population size falls dramatically.

4) A change in the population size of one species can have a huge knock on effect for other species — e.g. by disrupting food chains.

5) Therefore it's really important that we try to conserve (protect) species and habitats. There are already lots of conservation schemes set up to help us do this. For example:

Captive Breeding Programs

1) Species that are low in numbers in the wild can be bred in captivity to help increase their numbers — e.g. pandas.

2) Animals bred in captivity can then be reintroduced to the wild.

Fishing Quotas

1) Fish stocks are declining because we're overfishing — we're fishing too much.

2) This means there are fewer fish for us to eat, the ocean's food chains are affected and some species of fish may disappear altogether in some areas.

3) Fishing quotas are limits to the amounts of certain fish species that fishermen are allowed to catch.

Protected Areas

1) Protected areas includes places such as national parks and nature reserves.

2) They protect habitats by limiting the number of buildings that can be built, and limiting the amount of farming and other industry that can happen in the area.

Net profits — the money that a fisherman makes...

Humans are always taking things from the planet, creating pollution and disrupting other organisms. We need to manage what we're doing now so that the Earth isn't in too messed up for future generations.

Summary Questions

Section 5 is all about how living things manage to survive in their natural environment. They all need to find enough food to live on, and yet also avoid the multitude of other hazards that conspire to wipe them out.
The questions below are designed to see how well you've learned all the information in this section. Remember, you need to keep on practising these questions. If there's one you don't know the answer to, look back through the section, find out what it is, and then learn it for next time.

1) What exactly is an organism's habitat?

2) What word describes organisms that need each other to survive?

3) What is a food chain?

4) Give an example of a food chain.

5) What's the difference between a food chain and a food web?

6) Give definitions for all of the following terms:
   a) top carnivore,   b) tertiary consumer,   c) secondary consumer,
   d) primary consumer,   e) producer.

7) Look at the food web on page 35.
   a) What is likely to happen to the number of otters if all the pike die? Why?
   b) Suggest what may happen to the number of perch if the number of tadpoles increases. Explain your answer.

8) What happens to poisons as they are passed along a food chain?

9) What is an organism's environment?

10) What does it mean if an organism is adapted to its environment?

11) List three features of an Arctic hare which make it well adapted to its environment.

12) Describe how a cactus is adapted to desert conditions.

13) Name three daily changes which might affect plants and animals.

14) Give one way that an Arctic hare adapts to: a) daily changes,   b) seasonal changes.

15) Give one way that a cactus adapts to: a) daily changes,   b) seasonal changes.

16) What would you use to measure: a) light intensity?   b) temperature?

17) What does 'population' mean?

18) Give two factors that affect population size.

19) What is a quadrat?

20) Describe how you could use a quadrat to estimate the number of daffodils in a field.

21) What is sustainable development?

22) Explain how hunting one species may affect the population size of another species.

23) Explain what fishing quotas are and why they are important.

24) Other than fishing quotas, give two examples of conservation schemes.

Particle Theory

Particle theory — sounds pretty fancy. But actually it's pretty straightforward.

The **Three States of Matter** — *Solid, Liquid and Gas*

1) A material can be a <u>solid</u>, a <u>liquid</u> or a <u>gas</u> — these are called the three <u>states of matter</u>.

2) All <u>materials</u> are made up of <u>tiny particles</u>.

3) The <u>particles</u> in a substance stay the <u>same</u> whether it's a <u>solid</u>, a <u>liquid</u> or a <u>gas</u>.

4) What changes is the <u>arrangement</u> of the particles and their <u>energy</u>.

Solids — Particles are Held *Very Tightly Together*

1) There are <u>strong</u> forces of <u>attraction</u> between particles.

2) The particles are held closely in <u>fixed positions</u> in a very regular <u>arrangement</u>. But they do <u>vibrate</u> to and fro.

3) The particles <u>don't move</u> from their positions, so all solids keep a <u>definite shape</u> and <u>volume</u> — they can't <u>flow</u> like liquids.

4) Solids <u>can't</u> be compressed because the particles are <u>very closely packed</u>.

5) Solids are usually <u>very dense</u>, as they have <u>lots</u> of particles in a <u>small</u> volume.

Particles in a Solid

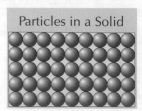

See page 88 for more about density.

Liquids — Particles are **Close Together** But They Can **Move**

1) There are <u>some</u> forces of <u>attraction</u> between the particles.

2) The particles are <u>close</u>, but free to <u>move</u> past each other — and they do <u>stick together</u>. The particles are <u>constantly</u> moving in all directions.

3) Liquids <u>don't</u> keep a <u>definite shape</u> and can form puddles. They <u>flow</u> and <u>fill the bottom</u> of a container. But they do keep the <u>same volume</u>.

4) Liquids <u>don't</u> compress easily as the particles are packed <u>closely together</u>.

5) Liquids are <u>quite dense</u>, as they have <u>quite a lot</u> of particles in a <u>small</u> volume.

Particles in a Liquid

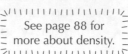

Gases — Particles are **Far Apart** and **Whizz About a Lot**

1) There are <u>very weak</u> forces of <u>attraction</u> between the particles.

2) The particles are <u>far apart</u> and free to <u>move</u> quickly in <u>all</u> directions.

3) The particles move <u>fast</u>, and so <u>collide</u> with each other and the <u>container</u>.

4) Gases <u>don't</u> keep a <u>definite shape</u> or <u>volume</u> and will always <u>expand to fill</u> any container. <u>Gases</u> can be <u>compressed easily</u> because there's a lot of free <u>space</u> between the particles.

5) Gases have <u>very low densities</u>, because there are <u>not many</u> particles in a <u>large</u> volume.

Particles in a Gas

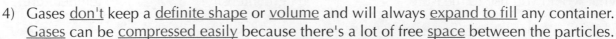

Every Substance has its own *Melting* and *Boiling Point*

1) The <u>melting point</u> of a material is the temperature at which it turns <u>from a solid to a liquid</u>.

2) Its <u>boiling point</u> is the temperature at which it turns <u>from a liquid to a gas</u>.

3) Every material has it own <u>individual</u> melting and boiling point — so you can use the melting point and boiling point to <u>identify</u> a substance (see pages 51 and 53).

More Particle Theory

Particle theory can be used to explain all sorts of exciting things, like, erm, gas pressure and diffusion. I say exciting. I may be exaggerating just a teensy tiny bit...

*Gas Pressure is Due to **Particles Hitting a Surface***

*Increasing the **Temperature** Increases Pressure*

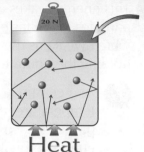

1) When you increase the temperature, it makes the particles move faster.

2) This has two effects:

> a) They hit the walls harder.
> b) They hit more often.

Increasing the temperature will only increase the pressure if the volume stays the same.

3) Both these things increase the pressure.

Heat

*Reducing the **Volume** Increases Pressure*

1) If you reduce the volume it makes the pressure increase.

2) This is because when the particles are squashed up into a smaller space they'll hit the walls more often.

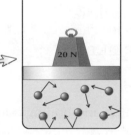

*Diffusion is Just Particles **Spreading Out***

1) Particles "want" to spread out — this process is called diffusion.

2) Diffusion can happen in liquids and gases.

3) An example of diffusion in a gas is when a smell spreads slowly through a room:

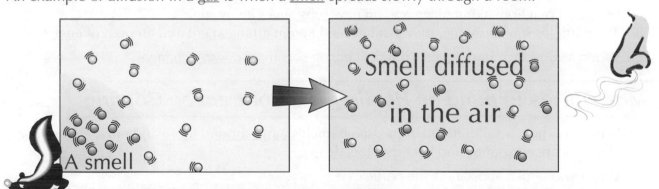

A smell · Smell diffused in the air

The smell particles move from an area of high concentration (i.e. where there are lots of them) to an area of low concentration (where there's only a few of them).

4) Diffusion is slow because the smell particles keep bumping into air particles, which stops them making forward progress and often sends them off in a completely different direction — it's a bit like trying to run blindfolded through a herd of frisky bullocks. As you do.

Let the information on this page diffuse into your mind...

...you know — move from where there's a high concentration of information (this page) to where there's a low concentration (err... your mind). To be honest though, you're going to need to be a bit more active when it comes to learning this. You know the drill. Look, cover and scribble it all down.

Changes of State

Changes of state don't change the particles — just their arrangement or their energy.

Changes of State — i.e. changing from one state of matter to another.

3 At a certain temperature, the particles have enough energy to break free from their positions. This is called melting — the solid turns into a liquid.

2 This makes the particles move more which weakens the forces that hold the solid together.

1 When a solid is heated, its particles gain more energy.

4 When a liquid is heated, the particles gain even more energy.

5 This energy makes the particles move faster, which weakens the forces holding the liquid together.

6 At a certain temperature, the particles have enough energy to break the forces. This is called boiling and the liquid turns into a gas.

Liquid

Solid

Gas

melting / freezing

boiling / condensing

subliming (rare)

Key: heat supplied | heat given out

Evaporation and boiling both describe a change from a liquid to a gas, but they're not quite the same. Evaporation can happen slowly at any temperature, but boiling occurs rapidly at a specific temperature.

Physical Changes Don't Involve a Change in Mass

1) Changing state is an example of a physical change.

2) Physical changes are different to chemical changes, because there's no actual reaction taking place and no new substances are made. The particles stay the same, they just have a different arrangement and amount of energy.

3) When a substance undergoes a physical change, its mass doesn't change.

Dissolving (see page 46) is another physical change.

Most Things Expand on Heating and Contract on Cooling

1) When you heat a solid, liquid or gas, the particles move around more and move further apart. The substance expands and becomes less dense.

2) When you cool a substance, the particles move around less and get closer together. The substance contracts and becomes more dense.

Ice is unusual though — when it melts, the particles move closer together and the density increases.

Thermometers Use the Expansion of Mercury or Alcohol

1) Mercury and some alcohols (like ethanol) are liquids at room temperature, so they are ideal for use in thermometers.

2) When a thermometer is heated, the liquid expands and moves up the tube (and vice versa).

Phew — another page of jostling snooker balls...*   *They're particles actually.

So your ice cream melts because the little snooker balls of ice cream take in energy, which means they can break free from their positions — so your ice cream becomes a liquid. But it still tastes nice.

Section 6 — Classifying Materials

The Periodic Table

If you've ever wondered what everything is made of, then the simple answer is atoms.

You Need to Know About **Atoms**...

1) Atoms are a type of <u>tiny</u>, <u>tiny</u>, <u>particle</u>. <u>All matter</u> is made up of <u>atoms</u>.

2) There are <u>different types</u> of atom, and each <u>element</u> (see below) contains a <u>different type</u>.

element → copper   iron   oxygen

one type of atom →

...and **Elements**

1) An <u>element</u> is a substance that contains <u>only one type</u> of <u>atom</u>.

2) It can't be <u>broken down</u> into anything simpler.

All Elements Have a **Name** and a **Symbol**

1) There are over <u>100 different elements</u> and writing their names out each time you wanted to mention one would take ages.

2) So each element has a <u>symbol</u> — usually of <u>one or two letters</u>.

3) This symbol can also be used to mean just <u>one atom</u> of that specific element.

4) You <u>need to know</u> the symbols for these elements.

Name	Symbol
hydrogen	H
helium	He
carbon	C
nitrogen	N
oxygen	O
sodium	Na
magnesium	Mg
sulfur	S
chlorine	Cl
calcium	Ca
iron	Fe
copper	Cu

The **Periodic Table** Lists **All** the **Elements**

1) The periodic table shows all the <u>elements</u> we have <u>discovered</u>.

2) <u>Elements</u> with <u>similar properties</u> are arranged into <u>vertical columns</u> in the table.

3) The <u>vertical columns</u> are called <u>groups</u>, and the <u>horizontal rows</u> are called <u>periods</u>.

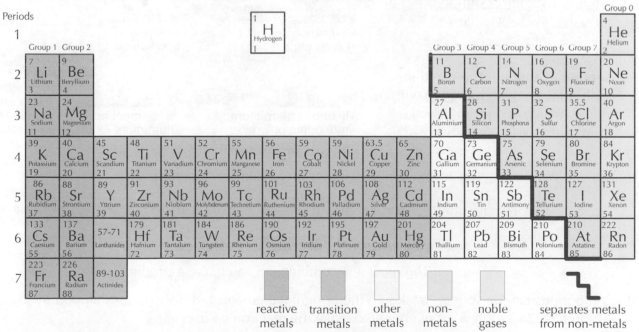

Anyone know any good jokes about sodium? Na...

I know, some of the symbols are a bit weird (like Fe for iron) — it's cos they're based on Latin words. Thankfully most of the ones in that list you need to know are pretty straightforward, like O for oxygen.

Compounds

Throw a few elements together and you end up with some compounds. Now things start to get exciting...

Compounds *Contain* **Two or More** *Elements* **Joined Up**

1) When <u>two or more atoms</u> join together, a <u>molecule</u> is made. The "<u>joins</u>" are known as <u>chemical bonds</u>.

2) <u>Compounds</u> are formed when atoms of <u>different elements</u> join together. Like in <u>carbon dioxide</u>, CO_2:

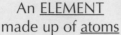

An <u>ELEMENT</u> made up of <u>atoms</u>	An <u>ELEMENT</u> made up of <u>molecules</u>	A <u>COMPOUND</u> made up of <u>molecules</u>	A <u>MIXTURE</u> of different <u>elements</u>

The atoms are all the same and not joined up — it must be an <u>element</u>.	The atoms are joined, but there's still only one type, so it's still an <u>element</u>.	Here we have different atoms joined together — that's a <u>compound</u> alright.	This is <u>not</u> a compound because the elements aren't joined up — it's a <u>mixture</u>.

Compounds *are Formed from* **Chemical Reactions**

1) In a <u>chemical reaction</u>, chemicals <u>combine together</u> or <u>split apart</u> to form <u>new substances</u>. The chemicals you <u>start with</u> are called <u>reactants</u>. The chemicals you <u>end up with</u> are called <u>products</u>.

2) When a <u>new</u> compound is <u>synthesised</u> (made), elements <u>combine</u>.

3) The <u>new compounds</u> produced by any chemical reaction are always totally <u>different</u> from the <u>original elements</u> (or reactants). The <u>classic example</u> of this is <u>iron</u> reacting with <u>sulfur</u> as shown below:

Iron is <u>magnetic</u>. It reacts with <u>sulfur</u> to make <u>iron sulfide</u>, a totally new substance which is <u>not magnetic</u>.

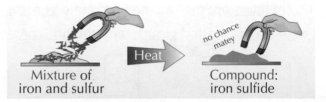

Mixture of iron and sulfur   Heat   no chance matey   Compound: iron sulfide

Another example is the reaction of <u>aluminium</u> (which is <u>grey</u>) with <u>iodine</u> (which is <u>purple</u>) to make <u>aluminium iodide</u> (which is <u>white</u>).

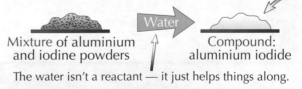

Mixture of aluminium and iodine powders   Water   Compound: aluminium iodide

The water isn't a reactant — it just helps things along.

This reaction needs to be carried out in a fume cupboard as you also get some nasty iodine gas given off.

4) You can write <u>equations</u> to <u>show what happens</u> in a chemical reaction.

Word equation: iron + sulfur ⟶ iron sulfide

In symbols: Fe + S ⟶ FeS

This is the formula for iron sulfide. There's more about formulae on the next page.

The <u>reactants</u> combine...   ...to make a <u>product</u>.

5) Compounds can be <u>split up</u> back into their <u>original</u> elements but it <u>won't</u> just happen by itself — you have to <u>supply</u> a lot of <u>energy</u> to make the reaction go in <u>reverse</u>.

Learn about compounds — and try and make it stick...

They really do like seeing if you know the difference between elements, compounds and mixtures. Make sure you do. There's more on page 46 about mixtures too — go have a nosy.

Compounds

When elements combine to make a compound, their names change slightly. Intrigued? Then read on...

All Compounds Have a **Chemical Formula**

1) All compounds have a chemical formula. It contains the symbols for the elements it's made from.

   E.g. iron sulfide contains the elements iron (Fe) and sulfur (S). Its formula is FeS.

2) Small numbers in a formula tell you if there's more than one atom present of a particular element.

   E.g. the formula for water is H_2O. It contains 2 hydrogen (H) atoms and 1 oxygen (O) atom.

Naming Compounds — **Two Simple Rules**

RULE 1: When two different elements combine the ending is usually "something -ide".

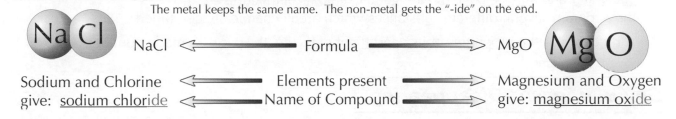

The metal keeps the same name. The non-metal gets the "-ide" on the end.

NaCl ⟵———— Formula ————⟶ MgO

Sodium and Chlorine ⟵—— Elements present ——⟶ Magnesium and Oxygen
give: sodium chloride ⟵——— Name of Compound ——⟶ give: magnesium oxide

Similarly: Sulfur → Sulfide   Iodine → Iodide   Bromine → Bromide   Fluorine → Fluoride

RULE 2: When three or more different elements combine and one of them is oxygen, the ending is be "something -ate".

The metal keeps the same name. The non-metal that isn't oxygen gets the "-ate" on the end. (The oxygen doesn't get a bit.)

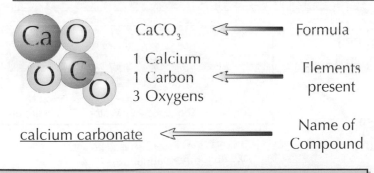

$CaCO_3$ ⟵——— Formula

1 Calcium
1 Carbon ⟵
3 Oxygens

Elements present

calcium carbonate ⟵——— Name of Compound

And in just the same way:

Sodium + Carbon + 3 Oxygens makes:
sodium carbonate

Potassium + Sulfur + 4 Oxygens makes:
potassium sulfate

...But There are **Exceptions** to These **Rules**

1) Unfortunately, not every compound follows these rules.

2) The table on the right gives a few other names of compounds that you need to be familiar with.

Compound	Formula
carbon dioxide	CO_2
hydrochloric acid (stomach acid)	HCl
methane (natural gas)	CH_4
sodium hydroxide	NaOH

There are two oxygen atoms, so you put 'di-' in front of the 'oxide' bit.

Technically it's called hydrogen chloride if it's a gas, but you'll only really find it as an acid.

This one's just a bit odd and doesn't follow Rule 2.

-ides and -ates — it's the game of the name, pal...

Naming compounds can get much more complicated than this — but for your exams you'll be fine as long as you learn the two simple rules in the boxes above plus the exceptions listed in the table.

Mixtures

A mixture in chemistry is a bit like a big salad — all the components are mixed up in a bowl, but you can pick out the olives if you really want to. You'll need to learn the technical terms too though...

Mixtures are Substances That are **NOT** Chemically *Joined Up*

1) A pure substance is made up of only one type of element OR only one type of compound. It can't be separated into anything simpler without a chemical reaction.

   E.g. pure water is made up of H_2O molecules only. These molecules can't be separated into H and O atoms without a chemical reaction.

2) A mixture contains two or more different substances. These substances aren't chemically joined up — so, if you're clever, you can separate them very easily using physical methods (i.e. without a chemical reaction). See pages 48 and 49 for more.

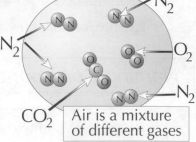
Air is a mixture of different gases

3) Sea water and air (see page 67) are good examples of mixtures — they contain several different substances which aren't chemically combined.

4) A mixture has the properties of its constituent parts (i.e. the parts it's made from).

Dissolving isn't *Disappearing*

1) Dissolving is one way of making a mixture.

2) When you add a solid (the solute) to a liquid (the solvent) the bonds holding the solute particles together sometimes break.

3) The solute particles can then mix with the molecules in the liquid forming a solution.

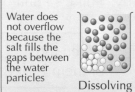
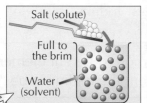

Salt (solute)
Full to the brim
Water (solvent)
Water does not overflow because the salt fills the gaps between the water particles
Solution
Dissolving
Dissolved

4) There are no chemical changes going on here — dissolving is a physical change (see page 42).

5) Remember, mass is conserved in a physical change. When the salt dissolves it doesn't vanish — it's still there.

20g Salt   Added to 100g Water =120g Solution

6) If you evaporated off the solvent (the water), you'd see the solute (the salt) again.

See page 48 for more about using evaporation to separate solutions.

You need to learn these seven definitions:

1) Solute – is the solid being dissolved.

2) Solvent – is the liquid it's dissolving into.

3) Solution – is a mixture of a solute and a solvent that does not separate out.

4) Soluble – means it will dissolve.

5) Insoluble – means it will not dissolve.

6) Saturated – a solution that you can't dissolve any more solute into.

7) Solubility – a measure of how much solute will dissolve.

This page is the solution to all your revision woes...

There's a lot of stuff on this page, but it's all really useful info that you need to remember for your exams, so you'd best get learning it. And be careful with all those sol- words, it's easy to muddle them up.

Solvents and Solutions

A whole page about solutions? Oh, I'm totally saturated with anticipation about this.

Saturation is when No More Solute will Dissolve in a Solvent

1) If you keep adding a solute to a solvent, eventually you'll reach the point where no more solute will dissolve — when this happens the solution is saturated.

2) Any more solute that you add will just sink to the bottom of the container.

Solubility Increases with Temperature

1) As temperature increases, the particles in the solvent have more energy and move faster.

2) The solvent particles bump into more solute molecules and break the bonds that hold them together.

3) So at higher temperatures more solute will dissolve in the solvent.

Solubility Varies Between Solvents

1) Different solutes are more soluble in some solvents than others. E.g.:
   - Nail varnish is insoluble in water but soluble in acetone (nail varnish remover).
   - At room temperature, you can dissolve around 350 g of sodium chloride in a litre of water. At the same temperature, you can only dissolve 15 g of sodium chloride in a litre of methanol.
2) When you're choosing a solvent, make sure it's suitable for the substance you're trying to dissolve.

A solvent's ability to dissolve a solute isn't the only thing to consider — some can be harmful.

For example, chlorinated hydrocarbons (like dichloromethane) are great solvents for loads of different substances. But they're also really toxic and bad for the environment.

Water is an Important Solvent...

1) Water is a very useful solvent, because it dissolves lots of solutes really easily.

2) It's essential in the human body (and in all other organisms) because important substances like sodium chloride and other nutrients and minerals dissolve in it and can be carried around the body.

3) It also dissolves and carries away waste products (like carbon dioxide) from cells.

...But There are Lots of Other Solvents Too

1) Alcohols such as ethanol can dissolve most compounds that water dissolves, but they can also dissolve some substances that water can't — like oils and fats.

2) This makes these alcohols very useful solvents in industry.

3) For example, ethanol is used as a solvent for perfume and aftershave. It can mix with both the oils (which give the smell) and the water (which makes up the bulk).

4) Acetone (also called propanone) is a useful solvent too. As well as being used as nail varnish remover, it's used in paint thinners and to dissolve superglue.

I can't think of anything funny to say about this page at all...

Tell you what — there's a cracker of a joke on page 92. Go and have a read of that to cheer yourself up. When you're feeling better, come back and start learning the stuff on the page. Cool beans.

Separating Mixtures

There are all sorts of ways you can separate mixtures. You've got to know about four of them.

1) Filtration   2) Evaporation   3) Chromatography   4) Distillation (see the next page).

All four make use of the different properties of the constituent parts to separate them out.

Filtration and *Evaporation* — Used to *Separate Out Rock Salt*

1) Rock salt is simply salt that's been dug out from underground. It has tiny bits of rock and sand mixed in with the solid salt (sodium chloride).

2) Salt dissolves in water but rock and sand don't. You can use this to separate them:

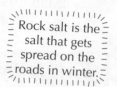
Rock salt is the salt that gets spread on the roads in winter.

You Need to *Learn* the *Four Steps* of the Method:

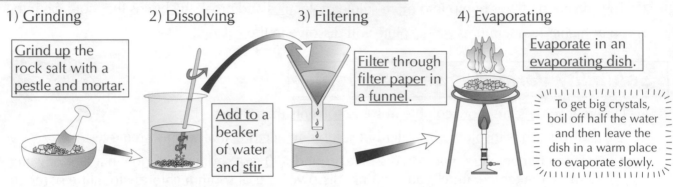

1) Grinding

Grind up the rock salt with a pestle and mortar.

2) Dissolving

Add to a beaker of water and stir.

3) Filtering

Filter through filter paper in a funnel.

4) Evaporating

Evaporate in an evaporating dish.

To get big crystals, boil off half the water and then leave the dish in a warm place to evaporate slowly.

• The sand and rock don't dissolve (they're insoluble) so they stay as grains. These grains won't fit through the tiny holes in the filter paper, so they collect on the paper — this is called the residue.

• The salt is dissolved in solution so it does go through. This solution is called the filtrate.

• When you evaporate off the water, crystals of salt form in the evaporating dish. This is crystallisation.

Chromatography is Ideal for Separating *Dyes*

1) Inks and food colourings are made up of mixtures of different dyes.

2) Chromatography uses a solvent soaking through filter paper to separate the dyes.

3) Different dyes wash through the paper at different speeds. Some stick to the paper more and move quite slowly, while others dissolve in the solvent more and travel through the paper quickly.

4) By looking at the results (called a chromatogram) you can compare the dyes in different substances.

METHOD 1

1) Put a dot of ink on a circle of filter paper.

2) Make a wick (a thin strip of paper hanging down into the solvent).

3) The solvent travels up the wick and washes the dyes through the paper.

filter paper
ink
wick

wick
water (solvent)

different dyes in the ink

If the dyes are insoluble in water, you'll have to use another solvent.

METHOD 2

1) Put spots of inks on a pencil baseline on filter paper.

2) Put the paper in a beaker with a little solvent at the bottom.

3) The solvent seeps up the paper, carrying the ink dyes with it.

4) Each dye will form a spot in a different place:

solvent

Spots A and D must be the same ink as they contain the same dyes.

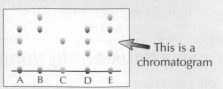
This is a chromatogram

A B C D E

Separating Mixtures

Simple Distillation *Separates* a *Solvent* from a *Solution*

1) <u>Simple distillation</u> is used to separate out mixtures of <u>liquids</u> and <u>solids</u>.

2) The liquid is <u>heated</u> and <u>evaporates</u> off as a gas, leaving the <u>solid</u> behind.

3) The gas is then passed into a <u>Liebig condenser</u> — this <u>cools</u> the gas, so it <u>condenses</u> back into a liquid.

4) Simple distillation is great for getting <u>pure water</u> back from something like <u>sea water</u> or <u>ink</u>.

Pure water in the beaker | Liquid ink mixture in the flask | Concentrated ink in the flask

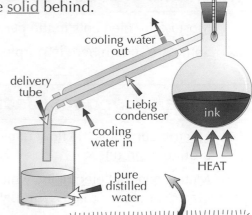

-10–100 °C thermometer

cooling water out

delivery tube

Liebig condenser

cooling water in

ink

HEAT

pure distilled water

After collecting the liquid, remove the delivery tube from the beaker before you turn off the heat. Otherwise, as the air inside the flask cools and contracts, some of the liquid can get sucked back into the flask.

Fractional Distillation *Separates* Mixed *Liquids*

1) <u>Fractional distillation</u> is used to separate mixtures of liquids.

2) <u>Different liquids</u> boil off at <u>different temperatures</u>, around their <u>own boiling point</u>.

3) A <u>fractionating column</u> ensures that only the liquid that <u>boils</u> at the temperature on the thermometer makes it to the top and escapes the column. Any other liquids will <u>condense</u> and run back <u>down</u> into the flask.

4) When each liquid has been <u>boiled off</u>, the temperature <u>rises</u> until the <u>next</u> fraction (liquid) starts to boil off. This means each fraction is <u>pure</u>.

5) <u>Ethanol</u> (alcohol) has a <u>lower boiling point</u> than <u>water</u>, so fractional distillation can be used to extract the ethanol from <u>wine</u> (to make stronger alcoholic drinks).

6) You can also use it to separate <u>crude oil</u> into petrol, diesel and other fuels.

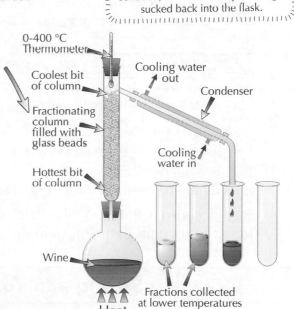

0-400 °C Thermometer

Coolest bit of column

Cooling water out

Condenser

Fractionating column filled with glass beads

Cooling water in

Hottest bit of column

Wine

Heat

Fractions collected at lower temperatures

Check *Purity* with *Freezing* and *Boiling Points*

1) A <u>pure</u> chemical substance has <u>fixed freezing and boiling points</u> — e.g. pure water boils at 100 °C and freezes at 0 °C. These figures are <u>known</u> for a huge range of substances.

2) This helps us to <u>identify unknown</u> substances, e.g. if a liquid boils at <u>exactly</u> 100 °C it's likely to be <u>pure</u> water.

3) <u>Impurities change</u> freezing and boiling points, e.g. impurities in water cause it to boil <u>above</u> 100 °C.

4) This means you can <u>test the purity</u> of a substance you've separated from a mixture.

Pure Substance	Freezing Point °C	Boiling Point °C
Water	0	100
Ethanol	-114	78
Aluminium	660	2520

Revise mixtures — just filter out the important bits...

Examiners love asking you about separation techniques (strange, I know), so make sure you've got all the facts and the diagrams absolutely 100% learnt. Make sure you know how to check purity too.

Section 6 — Classifying Materials

Properties of Metals

Metals are jolly useful. We use them all the time in bendy wires, bridges, musical instruments and more. So it's only fair that you learn these two pages of glorious facts about them in return...

1) *Metals* Can be Found in the *Periodic Table*

1) <u>Most</u> of the elements in the periodic table are metals.

2) Some are shown here in purple, to the <u>left</u> of the <u>zig zag</u>.

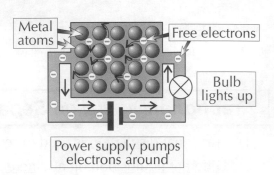

2) *Metals Conduct Electricity*

1) <u>Electric current</u> is the <u>flow</u> of <u>electrical charge</u> around a <u>circuit</u>.

2) Metals <u>conduct electricity</u>, which means they allow electrical charge to pass through them <u>easily</u>.

3) The moving charges are <u>negatively-charged</u> particles called <u>electrons</u>.

4) Metals contain some electrons that are <u>free to move</u> between the metal atoms. These free electrons can carry an electric current from <u>one end</u> of the metal to the <u>other</u>.

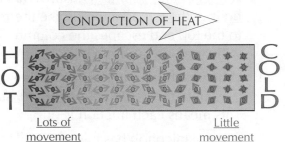

Power supply pumps electrons around

3) *Metals Conduct Heat*

1) This means metals let <u>thermal energy</u> pass through.

2) If you heat one end of a piece of metal, the "<u>hot</u>" particles will <u>vibrate strongly</u>.

3) Because the particles are very close together, the vibrations are easily <u>passed on</u> through the metal.

4) <u>Free electrons</u> in the metal also help to <u>transfer heat energy</u> from the <u>hot</u> parts of the metal to the <u>cooler</u> parts as they move around.

CONDUCTION OF HEAT

HOT — COLD

Lots of movement   Little movement

4) *Metals* are *Strong* and *Tough*

1) Metals have high <u>tensile strength</u> (they can be pulled hard without breaking).

2) This is because there are <u>strong forces</u> between metal atoms that <u>hold them together</u>.

3) So they make good <u>building materials</u>.

5) *Metals* are *Shiny*

<u>Polished</u> or <u>freshly cut</u> metals give strong <u>reflection</u> of light from their <u>smooth surface</u>. This makes them look <u>shiny</u>.

6) *Metals* are *Malleable*

1) Metals are <u>easily shaped</u> (malleable) because the atoms in metals can <u>slide over</u> each other.

2) This means metals can be <u>hammered</u> into <u>thin sheets</u> or <u>bent</u> — all <u>without shattering</u>.

Properties of Metals

7) Metals are Ductile

1) This means they can be drawn out into <u>wires</u>.

2) Metals <u>aren't brittle</u> like non-metals (see p. 53) are. They just <u>bend</u> and <u>stretch</u>.

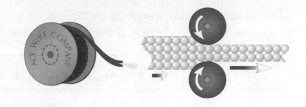

8) Metals have High Melting and Boiling Points

1) A <u>lot</u> of <u>heat energy</u> is needed to <u>melt</u> metals and even more to boil them.

2) This is because their <u>atoms</u> are joined by <u>strong</u> forces.

3) The table gives the <u>melting</u> and <u>boiling points</u> of some metals.

4) Most metals are <u>solids</u> at <u>room temperature</u>. <u>Mercury</u> is the only exception. It's a <u>liquid</u> at room temperature.

Metal	Melting Point (°C)	Boiling Point (°C)
Aluminium	660	2520
Copper	1085	2562
Magnesium	650	1090
Iron	1538	2861
Zinc	420	907

9) Metals have High Densities

1) <u>Density</u> is all to do with how much <u>stuff</u> there is squeezed into a certain <u>space</u>. (See page 88 for more about density.)

2) Metals feel <u>heavy</u> for their <u>size</u> (they're <u>very dense</u>) because they have a lot of <u>atoms</u> tightly packed into a <u>small volume</u>.

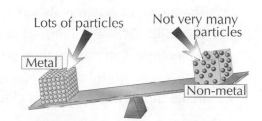

Lots of particles   Not very many particles

Metal   Non-metal

10) Metals Make Alloys When Mixed with Other Metals

1) A <u>combination</u> of different metals is called an <u>alloy</u>. The <u>properties</u> of the metals get <u>jumbled up</u> in the new <u>alloy</u>.

2) So <u>lighter, weaker metals</u> can be <u>mixed</u> with <u>heavier, stronger metals</u> and the <u>result</u> is, hopefully, an <u>alloy</u> which is <u>light and strong</u>.

Alloy Wheels — light and strong

11) Some Metals are Magnetic

1) Only <u>certain metals</u> are magnetic.

2) <u>Most</u> metals <u>aren't magnetic</u>. <u>Iron</u>, <u>nickel</u> and <u>cobalt</u> are.

3) <u>Alloys</u> made with these three metals will also be magnetic — e.g. <u>steel</u> is made mostly from <u>iron</u>, so is also <u>magnetic</u>.

Iron or nickel or cobalt (or an alloy containing one of them)

12) Metal Oxides are Alkaline

1) Metals react with <u>oxygen</u> to make <u>metal oxides</u>.

E.g. iron + oxygen ⟶ iron oxide

2) When a metal oxide is added to water, the solution has a <u>pH</u> which is <u>higher than 7</u> — i.e. it's <u>alkaline</u> (see page 59).

3) So <u>metal oxides</u> react with <u>acids</u> to make a <u>salt</u> and <u>water</u>.

There's loads more info about metal oxides on page 64.

Good Alloys — you can rely on friends from Birmingham...

Two pages of facts about metals just waiting to be soaked up into that giant sponge lurking between your ears. Keep practising till you can write out the headings from both pages, then write out the details.

Properties of Non-Metals

The properties of non-metal elements vary quite a lot.
Good — life would stink if everything was like sulfur...

1) *Non-metals* Can be Found in the *Periodic Table*

1) All the non-metals (with the exception of hydrogen) are clustered in the corner over on the <u>right</u> of the <u>zig zag</u>.
   Look, right over there.

2) There are <u>fewer</u> non-metals than metals.

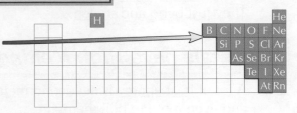

2) *Non-metals* are *Poor Conductors* of *Electricity*

1) Most non-metals are <u>electrical insulators</u>, which means that they <u>don't conduct electricity</u>.

2) The atoms in non-metals are <u>arranged</u> so that <u>electrons</u> (negative charges) <u>can't move</u> through them.

3) If electrons can't move then <u>no electric current flows</u>.

4) This is <u>very useful</u> — you can use non-metals to make things like <u>plugs</u> and electric cable <u>coverings</u>.

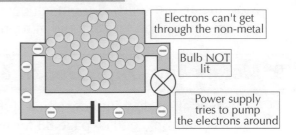

One exception to this rule is <u>graphite</u> — a <u>non-metal</u> made purely from <u>carbon atoms</u>. Its atoms are arranged in layers, which allow electrons to move along them, so graphite <u>can conduct electricity</u>.

3) *Non-metals* are *Poor Conductors* of *Heat*

1) <u>Heat</u> does <u>not</u> travel very well at all through non-metals.

2) If you heat one end of a non-metal, the "<u>hot</u>" particles <u>don't</u> pass on their <u>vibrations</u> very well.

3) This makes non-metals really good <u>thermal insulators</u> (<u>insulators</u> of <u>heat</u>).

4) That's why non-metals are used to make things like saucepan handles.

4) *Non-metals* are *NOT Strong* or *Hard-Wearing*

1) The <u>forces</u> between the particles in most <u>non-metals</u> are <u>weak</u> — this means they <u>break</u> easily.

2) It's also easy to <u>scrub</u> atoms or molecules off them — so they <u>wear away</u> quickly.

5) *Non-metals* are *Dull*

1) Most non-metals don't <u>reflect</u> light very well at all. Their surfaces are not usually as <u>smooth</u> as metals.

2) This makes them look <u>dull</u>.

Properties of Non-Metals

6) *Non-metals* are *Brittle*

1) Non-metal structures are held together by weak forces.

2) This means they can shatter all too easily.

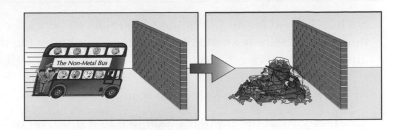

7) *Most* **Non-metals** *Have* **Low Melting** *and* **Boiling Points**

1) The forces which hold the particles in non-metals together are usually very weak. This means they melt and boil very easily.

2) The table gives the melting and boiling points of some non-metal elements.

3) At room temperature, most non-metal elements are gases or solids. Only one (bromine) is a liquid.

Non-Metal	Melting Point ($^{\circ}$C)	Boiling Point ($^{\circ}$C)
Sulfur	113	445
Oxygen	-218	-183
Chlorine	-101	-35
Helium	-272	-269
Neon	-249	-246
Bromine	-7	59

8) *Non-metals* Have *Low Densities*

1) Obviously the non-metals which are gases have very low densities.

2) This means they don't have very many particles packed into a certain space.

3) Some of these gases will even float in air — ideal for party balloons.

4) Even the liquid and solid non-metals have low densities.

9) *Non-metals* are *Not Magnetic*

1) Only a few metals like iron, nickel and cobalt are magnetic.

2) All non-metals are most definitely non-magnetic.

Sulfur

10) *Non-metal* Oxides are *Acidic*

1) Non-metals react with oxygen to make oxides. ⟶ E.g. carbon + oxygen ⟶ carbon dioxide

2) When a non-metal oxide is added to water, the solution has a pH which is below 7 — i.e. it's acidic (see page 59).

3) So non-metal oxides will react with alkalis to make a salt and water.

Non-Metals — they really are dull aren't they...

You still have to learn all about them though. Do it like this: Cover both of the last two pages with a bit of paper and try and write down each of the 10 subsections, one at a time. Start with page 52. Lower the paper each time to see if you scribbled it all down right. Keep trying till you can get them all.

Section 6 — Classifying Materials

Summary Questions

Section 6 is all about Classifying Materials so here's a whole page of delicious Summary Questions to help you classify how much you know. You know the drill: work through these questions and try to answer them. For any you can't do, look back through the section to find the answer — then learn it.

1) What are the three states of matter? Describe the main properties of each of them.

2) Draw what the particles look like in a solid, a liquid and a gas.

3) What is the 'melting point' of a substance?

4) What happens to the pressure of a fixed volume of gas if the temperature of the gas is increased?

5) Explain what diffusion is.

6) Give the names of five changes of state, and say which state they go from and to.

7) A substance changes from a liquid to a solid. During this change of state, will the substance need heat energy supplied to it, or will it release heat energy?

8) Does a change of state involve a change in mass?

9) What is an atom?

10) What is an element? Roughly how many elements are there in the periodic table?

11) Using the periodic table, give the chemical symbol for each of these:
a) sodium   b) magnesium   c) oxygen   d) iron   e) sulfur
f) nitrogen   g) carbon   h) chlorine   i) calcium   j) copper.

12) What is the 'join' between two atoms in a compound called?

13) What is a compound? How is a compound different from a mixture?

14) When you're doing a chemical reaction, what are the chemicals that you start with called?

15) Give one way that iron sulfide is different from a mixture of iron and sulfur.

16) Write the word equation for a reaction between hydrogen and oxygen that produces water.

17)* Give the names of each of the following compounds:
a) MgO b) CO_2 c) $NaCl$ d) $CaCO_3$ e) $NaOH$.

18)* Give the name of the compound you would get from chemically joining these elements:
a) sodium with chlorine   b) magnesium with chlorine   c) magnesium with carbon and oxygen.

19) What is a pure substance? What is a mixture?

20) Give the definition of each of the following words: a) solute   b) solvent   c) solution.

21) What word is used to describe a solution if no more solute can dissolve into it?

22) What happens to solubility when the temperature increases?

23) Why is water an important solvent?

24) Give one use for acetone (propanone).

25) This question is about separating mixtures of substances.
a) Describe how you could separate out rock salt to get pure salt crystals.
b) Which separation method would you use to separate out the different dyes in an ink?
c) Which separation method would you use to separate a mixture of liquids?

26) Out of metals and non-metals, which are the:
a) best electrical conductors   b) most brittle   c) shiniest   d) best thermal insulators?

27) Are metal oxides alkaline or acidic? What about non-metal oxides?

Everyday Chemical Reactions

OK then, time for a new section. And this one's a real humdinger...

Chemical Reactions are Really Important

1) Pretty much <u>all the materials</u> around us have been <u>made</u> by some sort of <u>chemical reaction</u>.

2) That includes both <u>non-organic</u> stuff and materials in <u>living systems</u>.
   These are all <u>examples</u> of things made by chemical reactions:

   - the <u>rust</u> on a garden spade
   - <u>carbon dioxide</u> in the air
   - the <u>acid</u> in your stomach
   - the <u>water</u> in your cells

3) Chemical reactions are <u>always going on</u> around us too. Here are some examples of chemical reactions that you might see happening at home:

   - <u>frying</u> an egg
   - <u>superglue hardening</u>
   - a banana <u>ripening</u>
   - <u>burning</u> candles

4) <u>Heating</u> a substance often causes a <u>chemical reaction</u> to occur.
   For example, <u>heating copper in oxygen</u> forms a new compound — <u>copper oxide</u>.

5) Some substances <u>don't react</u> when they're heated though — for example once you've made <u>copper oxide</u>, heating it further <u>doesn't do anything else</u>.

Bunsen Burners are Used for Heating in the Lab

1) Many <u>chemical reactions</u> need <u>heat</u> to get them going —
   you can use a <u>Bunsen burner</u> to provide the heat.

2) Bunsen burners burn <u>methane gas</u> and provide a <u>consistent</u> and <u>adjustable</u> heat source.

3) They have an <u>air hole</u> that can be <u>opened</u> or <u>closed</u> by different amounts to vary the amount of <u>oxygen</u> that enters the burner. This affects the <u>colour</u> and <u>temperature</u> of the flame.

4) A Bunsen burner can produce three different types of flame:

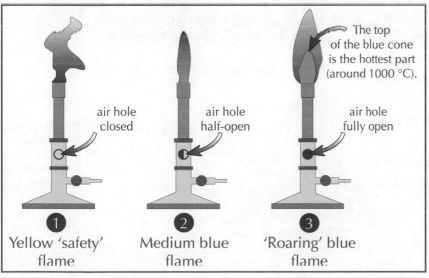

The top of the blue cone is the hottest part (around 1000 °C).

air hole closed — air hole half-open — air hole fully open

1 Yellow 'safety' flame — 2 Medium blue flame — 3 'Roaring' blue flame

1 <u>Yellow 'safety' flame</u>
This is what you set the burner to when you're not using it. This <u>isn't</u> used for heating as it makes too much soot.

2 <u>Medium blue flame</u>
This is what you use for <u>gentle heating</u>. It's hotter than the safety flame but not as hot as the roaring blue flame.

3 <u>'Roaring' blue flame</u>
This is what you use for <u>vigorous heating</u>. It's the <u>hottest</u> flame.

Flames, buns an' burgers — all you need for a good BBQ...

You've probably used a Bunsen burner in chemistry experiments — or you will pretty soon.
Just remember the three different types of flame, what each one is used for and how to make them.
Then you'll be able to carry out all sorts of weird and wonderful chemical reactions.

More on Chemical Reactions

In a chemical reaction, all that's really happening is the atoms are moving around into new formations. The reactants might give off heat, make a loud bang, or do a little dance, but the mass won't change.

Atoms Rearrange Themselves in a Chemical Reaction

1) In a chemical reaction atoms are not created or destroyed.

2) The atoms at the start of a reaction are still there at the end.

3) Bonds get broken and made in the reaction, as atoms rearrange themselves in going from the reactants to the products (p. 44). But the atoms themselves are not altered.

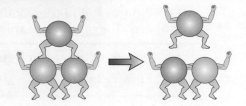

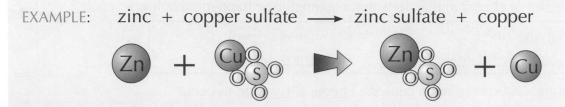

EXAMPLE: zinc + copper sulfate ⟶ zinc sulfate + copper

Zn + Cu O S O O ▶ Zn O S O O + Cu

The Mass Doesn't Change in a Chemical Reaction

1) In a chemical reaction no mass is lost or gained when the reactants turn into the products.

2) This is because the total number of atoms is the same before and after the reaction.

3) Chemical reactions involve a change in energy, i.e. reactions always give out or take in energy. This is usually heat energy, which causes the temperature in a reaction to go up or down.

4) Visible changes can occur in the reaction mixture.
   These show that a reaction has taken place, and a new substance has been formed.
   E.g. — bubbles of gas are given off, a solid is made, or the colour changes.

EXAMPLE: When magnesium reacts with blue copper sulfate solution, the solution becomes colourless, copper coats the magnesium strip and the temperature rises. But the mass stays the same.

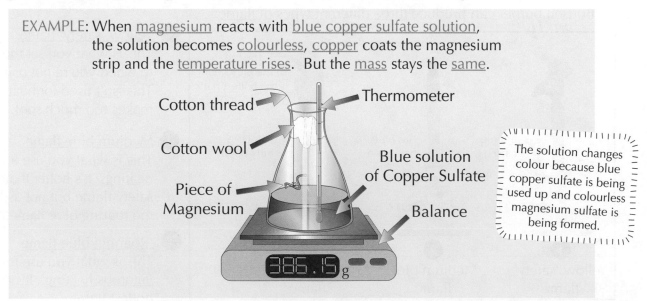

Cotton thread — Thermometer
Cotton wool
Piece of Magnesium
Blue solution of Copper Sulfate
Balance
386.15 g

The solution changes colour because blue copper sulfate is being used up and colourless magnesium sulfate is being formed.

Chemical reactions — just a case of atomic acrobatics...

Some chemical reactions involve colour changes, heating up, stinky fumes and even explosions, but there's one thing that always stays the same — the total mass, before and after the reaction. Get your head round that and you've basically solved all of chemistry. OK, maybe that's a slight exaggeration...

Oxidation

Two common examples of chemical reactions coming right up... just what the doctor ordered.

Oxidation is the Gain of Oxygen

1) When a substance <u>reacts</u> and <u>combines</u> with <u>oxygen</u>, it's called an <u>oxidation</u> reaction.

2) <u>Combustion</u> (see below) is an example of an oxidation reaction.

3) Another example of oxidation is <u>rusting</u>. <u>Iron</u> reacts with <u>oxygen</u> in the air to form <u>iron oxide</u>, i.e. <u>rust</u>.

iron + oxygen $\longrightarrow$ iron oxide (rust)

Combustion is Burning in Oxygen

1) Combustion is <u>burning</u> — it's when a <u>fuel</u> reacts with <u>oxygen</u> to release <u>energy</u>.

2) <u>Three</u> things are needed for combustion — <u>fuel</u>, <u>heat</u> and <u>oxygen</u>.

You Can Burn Some Elements in Oxygen

Here are <u>four examples</u>:

CARBON	Carbon will burn in oxygen if it's <u>very strongly heated</u>. It burns with an <u>orange flame</u> and produces <u>carbon dioxide</u> gas.

carbon + oxygen $\longrightarrow$ carbon dioxide

SULFUR	<u>Sulfur</u> burns in oxygen with a <u>pale blue flame</u> and produces <u>sulfur dioxide</u> gas.

sulfur + oxygen $\longrightarrow$ sulfur dioxide

IRON	<u>Iron</u> burns in oxygen if it's <u>heated very strongly</u>. It burns with an <u>orange flame</u> and produces black <u>iron oxide</u> powder.

iron + oxygen $\longrightarrow$ iron oxide

MAGNESIUM	Magnesium burns in oxygen with a <u>bright white flame</u>, forming white <u>magnesium oxide</u> powder.

magnesium + oxygen $\longrightarrow$ magnesium oxide

We Burn Hydrocarbons for Energy

1) <u>Hydrocarbons</u> are <u>fuels</u> containing only <u>hydrogen</u> and <u>carbon</u> (e.g. <u>methane</u>). When there's enough <u>heat</u> and <u>oxygen</u>, hydrocarbons <u>combust</u> (burn) to give <u>water</u> and <u>carbon dioxide</u>:

methane + oxygen $\longrightarrow$ carbon dioxide + water (+ energy)

2) This useful because it gives off <u>energy</u> in the form of <u>heat</u> and <u>light</u>. It's the process behind candles, wood fires, car engines, coal power plants, etc.

You Can Test for Oxygen and Carbon Dioxide

There's a test for water on the next page too.

OXYGEN

Oxygen <u>relights</u> a <u>glowing splint</u>.

Glowing splint

Oxygen

CARBON DIOXIDE

Carbon dioxide <u>turns limewater cloudy</u> — just bubble the gas through a test tube of limewater and watch what happens.

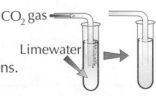

CO$_2$ gas

Limewater

Oxide (adj) — having big round eyes, like those of an ox...

Lots of oxidation reactions for you to learn here, plus two important chemical tests. Make sure you know the reactants and products of each reaction. Once you know them, treat yourself to a cookie.

Reduction and Thermal Decomposition

You've met oxidation — now meet its evil twin, reduction...

Reduction is the Removal of Oxygen From a Substance

1) Reduction is the opposite of oxidation — a reduction reaction is a loss of oxygen from a compound.

2) Reduction is used to extract metals from their ores which contain metal oxides.

3) For example, iron oxide can be reduced by carbon to produce pure iron (and carbon dioxide).

> iron oxide + carbon ⟶ iron + carbon dioxide

4) There's more on extracting metals from ores on page 62.

Thermal Decomposition is Breaking Down With Heat

1) Thermal decomposition is when a substance breaks down into two or more new substances when heated.

2) Some metal carbonates break down on heating. Carbonates are substances with CO_3 in them, like copper(II) carbonate ($CuCO_3$) and zinc carbonate ($ZnCO_3$).

3) They break down into a metal oxide (e.g. copper oxide, CuO) and carbon dioxide. This usually results in a colour change.

> EXAMPLE: The thermal decomposition of copper(II) carbonate.
> copper(II) carbonate ⟶ copper(II) oxide + carbon dioxide
> This is green... ...and this is black.

4) Hydrated metal compounds can also be broken down on heating.

5) They break down into anhydrous metal compounds and water. You will also usually see a colour change as the reaction happens.

Hydrated means that the substance contains some water. Anhydrous substances don't contain any water.

> EXAMPLE: The thermal decomposition of hydrated copper sulfate.
> hydrated copper sulfate ⟶ anhydrous copper sulfate + water
> This is blue... ...and this is white.

> EXAMPLE: The thermal decomposition of hydrated cobalt chloride.
> hydrated cobalt chloride ⟶ anhydrous cobalt chloride + water
> This is pink... ...and this is blue.

TESTING FOR WATER

These colour changes can be used to test for water. Water will:
• turn white anhydrous copper sulfate blue
• turn blue cobalt chloride paper pink.

6) There's one more example you need to know — how potassium permanganate breaks down on heating:

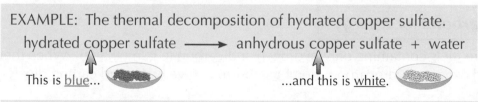

> EXAMPLE: The thermal decomposition of potassium permanganate.
> potassium permanganate ⟶ potassium manganate + manganese dioxide + oxygen
> This is purple... ...and this is green.

This page is easy — let me break it down for you...

Here are two more common types of chemical reaction to read up on and learn. You need to know all those examples of thermal decomposition too, including the different colour changes.

Acids and Alkalis

The pH scale is what scientists use to describe how acidic or alkaline a substance is.
An indicator takes on a colour based on the pH of the substance it's mixed with.

The pH Scale Shows the Strength of Acids and Alkalis

1) The pH scale goes from 0 to 14.

2) Anything with a pH below 7 is an acid. The strongest acid has pH 0.

3) Anything with a pH above 7 is an alkali. The strongest alkali has pH 14.

4) A neutral substance has pH 7 (e.g. water).

These are the colours that Universal indicator solution (see below) turns in the presence of acids and alkalis.

pH 0 1 2 3 4 5 6 7 8 9 10 11 12 13 14

Strong acids   Weak acids ┊ Weak alkalis   Strong alkalis
Neutral

Sulfuric acid
Citric acid
Rain water
Water
Pixie Washing up Liquid
Soap flakes
Jeff Cleaner
Sodium hydroxide solution
Hydrochloric acid
Acid rain
Washing-up liquid
Ammonia solution

Indicators Are Special Dyes Which Change Colour

1) An indicator is something that changes colour depending on whether it's in an acid or in an alkali.

2) Litmus paper is quite a popular indicator. Acids turn litmus paper red and alkalis turn it blue.

3) Litmus paper is useful, but it only tells you whether a liquid is acidic or alkaline, not how strong it is.

4) Some plants contain naturally occurring pH indicators that you can extract and use.

5) For example, if you chop up red cabbage and boil it in water, the solution you get can be used as a pH indicator. It will turn red in acids, purple in neutral solutions and turquoise or yellow in alkalis.

6) Universal indicator solution is a mixture of dyes which gives the range of colours shown above.

EXAMPLE Using Universal indicator to test the pH of an unknown solution.

1) Use a dropper to put a few drops of the solution on a white dimple tile.

2) Add a few drops of Universal indicator.

3) Match the colour to a pH chart.

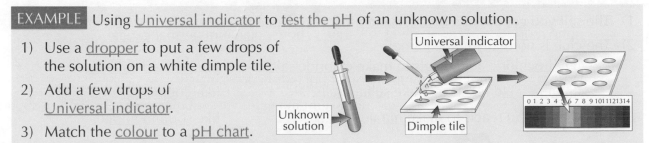

Universal indicator

Unknown solution

Dimple tile

0 1 2 3 4 5 6 7 8 9 10 11 12 13 14

---

pHew — the end of another page...

All of the items above are positioned below their actual pH on the pH scale. Make sure you know where they go — you don't want to get acid rain mixed up with soap flakes. That sounds painful...

Section 7 — Chemical Changes

Neutralisation Reactions

Make sure you learn all this stuff — it's pretty easy and a super-useful thing to know about.

Acids and Alkalis Neutralise Each Other

1) Acids react with alkalis to form a neutral solution of a salt and water:

$$acid + alkali \longrightarrow salt + water$$

2) This is known as a neutralisation reaction because the products have a neutral pH, i.e. a pH of 7.

3) There's a special case — if the alkali is a metal carbonate, this reaction also produces carbon dioxide.

$$acid + metal\ carbonate \longrightarrow salt + water + carbon\ dioxide$$

Making Salts by Neutralisation is Easy

1) Wearing eye protection, add an acid to an alkali dropwise with a pipette.

2) After every few drops, remove a small sample to check if the pH is neutral (pH 7).

3) Keep adding acid until the solution is neutral.

4) When it's neutral the solution is put in an evaporating dish and about two thirds of it can be boiled off to make a saturated solution of the salt.

A saturated salt solution can't have any more salt dissolved in it. See p. 47.

5) Leave this solution overnight for the rest of the water to evaporate and nice big salt crystals will form. The slower the crystallisation, the bigger the crystals.

EXAMPLE Reacting sodium hydroxide with hydrochloric acid to make sodium chloride.

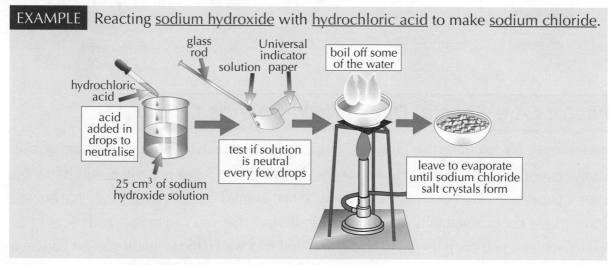

To Change the Salt, You Must Change the Acid

1) The salt you get out of a neutralisation reaction depends on the acid you use.

2) The clue is normally in the name:

Hydrochloric acid reacts to make chloride salts...   like sodium chloride.

Sulfuric acid reacts to make sulfate salts...   like copper sulfate.

Nitric acid reacts to make nitrate salts...   like sodium nitrate.

It's fun making salts — but I wouldn't put them on yer chips...

Make sure you know which kinds of salts you get from which kind of acid. I could tell you that if you don't learn this stuff it'll come up at the worst possible opportunity, and that without knowing the simple stuff on this page you'll get nowhere... but that would just be rubbing salt into the wound.

Useful Neutralisation Reactions

Neutralisation reactions don't just make pretty crystals in the lab — they're used for all sorts of things...

Indigestion is a Pain in the Chest

1) Indigestion can be caused by having too much hydrochloric acid in the stomach.

2) To remove it, the excess acid must be neutralised with a medium-strength base like magnesium oxide.

3) Strong alkalis like sodium hydroxide can't be used for indigestion tablets — because only a little too much would send the pH way too high.

4) This would affect the activity of enzymes in the stomach — so food would NOT be digested properly. It could also damage the stomach itself.

5) When you take indigestion tablets, the base in the tablets neutralises the excess acid, forming a salt and water in your stomach.

> A base is a substance that will react with an acid to neutralise it. An alkali is a base that is soluble in water. So an alkali is just a special type of base.

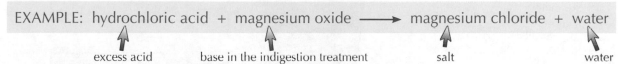

EXAMPLE: hydrochloric acid + magnesium oxide ⟶ magnesium chloride + water

excess acid — base in the indigestion treatment — salt — water

Acid Soil can Reduce Plant Growth

1) Soil can be acidic either because of acid rain or because of naturally acidic minerals in local rocks.

2) Certain plants prefer acid soils and others prefer neutral or alkaline soils.

3) The fact is that plants are fussy — the wrong pH means poor growth.

4) "Liming" acidic soil (adding a base to it) neutralises the acid and gets the pH just right for plants that want neutral or alkaline soil.

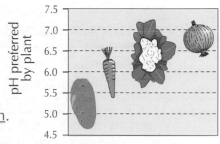

EXAMPLE: sulfuric acid + calcium hydroxide ⟶ calcium sulfate + water

in acid rain — a base — "lime" — salt — water

Ammonia Can Be Neutralised to Make Fertiliser

1) Ammonia dissolves in water to make an alkaline solution. When it reacts with nitric acid, you get a neutral salt — ammonium nitrate:

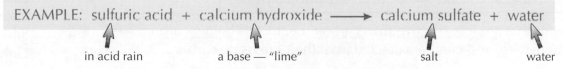

nitric acid + ammonia ⟶ ammonium nitrate

acid — base — salt

> This is a bit different from most neutralisation reactions because there's NO WATER produced — just the ammonium salt.

2) Ammonium nitrate can be added to soil to act as a source of nitrogen for plants.

3) Plants need nitrogen to make proteins. Farmers use fertilisers containing nitrogen on their fields to increase crop yields.

Good food is like homework — too much and you feel ill...

More information to be pummelled into your head. There's nothing for it but to sit down and learn it I'm afraid. Cheer up — you're nearly at the end of the section now (that may be a slight exaggeration).

Reactivity Series and Metal Extraction

You need to know which metals are most reactive — and which are least reactive.

The **Reactivity Series** — How **Well** a Metal **Reacts**

The Reactivity Series lists metals in order of their reactivity towards other substances.

Make sure you learn this list:

Carbon and hydrogen are non-metals, but it's useful to know where they are in the reactivity series (see below and pages 63-64).

REACTIVITY SERIES		
Potassium	K	Very Reactive
Sodium	Na	
Calcium	Ca	
Magnesium	Mg	Fairly Reactive
Aluminium	Al	
(CARBON)		
Zinc	Zn	Not Very Reactive
Iron	Fe	
Lead	Pb	
(HYDROGEN)		
Copper	Cu	
Silver	Ag	Not At All Reactive
Gold	Au	

Some **Metals** Can Be **Extracted** With **Carbon**

1) Metals are usually mined as ores (rocks containing metal compounds, like metal oxides).

2) A metal can be extracted from its ore by reduction using carbon. When an ore is reduced, oxygen is removed from it. E.g. the oxygen is removed from iron oxide to extract the iron:

iron oxide + carbon ⟶ iron + carbon dioxide

3) Only metals that are less reactive than carbon (i.e. metals below carbon in the reactivity series) can be extracted from their ore using carbon.

4) More reactive metals than carbon need to be extracted using other chemical reactions.

5) Some metals, like silver and gold, are so unreactive that they're often found in their pure form.

Potassium
Sodium
Calcium
Magnesium
Aluminium
—CARBON—
Zinc
Iron
Lead
Copper
Silver
Gold

The **Uses** of a **Metal** Can Depend on its **Reactivity**

1) Silver and gold don't corrode easily at all, so they're ideal for making jewellery and electrical contacts.

2) Other unreactive metals like lead and copper are used for roofing and piping because they don't corrode (break down) when exposed to air and water.

3) Iron is used in construction, but since it's more reactive, it rusts easily in water and air (see p. 67). One way to prevent rusting is to coat the iron with a barrier to keep out the water and oxygen:
   - Painting/Coating with plastic — ideal for big and small structures. It can be decorative too.
   - Oiling/Greasing — this has to be used when moving parts are involved, like on bike chains.

Metal extraction — sounds painful...

One of the first things you should know about metals is how reactive they all are — this is pretty basic stuff. So have a look at the reactivity series, then cover it up and try to write it all down from memory.

Reaction of Metals with Acids

Another page on metals to test your mettle — it's not so bad though, I promise. You don't need to learn each individual reaction, just how the reactivity of a metal affects how it reacts. Simple, no?

Reacting Metals With **Dilute Acid**

$$\text{metal} + \text{acid} \longrightarrow \text{salt} + \text{hydrogen}$$

All acids contain hydrogen — so the hydrogen here comes from the acid.

1) Metals above <u>hydrogen</u> in the <u>reactivity series</u> (see previous page) will <u>react</u> with <u>acids</u> to make a <u>salt</u> and <u>hydrogen</u>.

2) The metals <u>below</u> hydrogen in the <u>reactivity series don't react</u> with <u>acids</u>.

3) The reaction becomes <u>less and less exciting</u> as you go <u>down</u> the <u>series</u>.

More Reactive Metals React More **Violently**

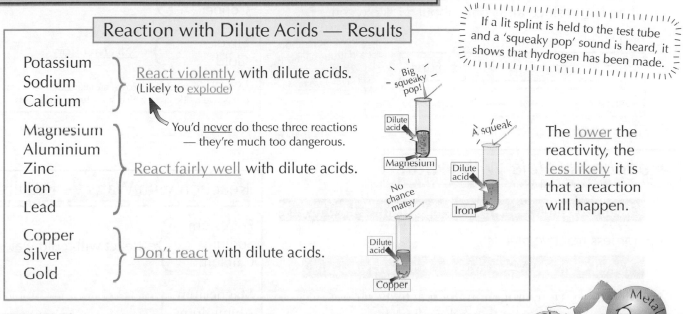

Reaction with Dilute Acids — Results

If a lit splint is held to the test tube and a 'squeaky pop' sound is heard, it shows that hydrogen has been made.

Potassium
Sodium
Calcium
} <u>React violently</u> with dilute acids. (Likely to <u>explode</u>)

You'd <u>never</u> do these three reactions — they're much too dangerous.

Magnesium
Aluminium
Zinc
Iron
Lead
} <u>React fairly well</u> with dilute acids.

Copper
Silver
Gold
} <u>Don't react</u> with dilute acids.

The <u>lower</u> the reactivity, the <u>less likely</u> it is that a reaction will happen.

EXAMPLES:

a) zinc + sulfuric acid $\longrightarrow$ zinc sulfate + hydrogen

$$Zn + H_2SO_4 \longrightarrow ZnSO_4 + H_2$$

The zinc <u>takes the place</u> of the hydrogen in the acid because it's <u>more reactive</u> than the hydrogen.

b) magnesium + hydrochloric acid $\longrightarrow$ magnesium chloride + hydrogen

$$Mg + 2HCl \longrightarrow MgCl_2 + H_2$$

The magnesium <u>takes the place</u> of the hydrogen in the acid — again because it's <u>more reactive</u> than the hydrogen.

c) If you put <u>copper</u> in dilute acid, nothing happens because it's <u>less reactive</u> than the hydrogen.

You're probably bored of metals now — time to reactivate...

It might seem like there's loads going on here, but really it's just the same principle repeated over and over. All the metals have roughly the same reaction with acids, some are just more violent than others (and some don't happen at all). All you need to know is the order of violentness. Is that a word?

Reactions of Metals with Oxygen and Water

Right, so the previous page was all about how metals react with acids. But you also need to know how metals react with oxygen and with water. By a happy coincidence, that's what this page is about.

Reacting Metals With **Oxygen**

Metal + Oxygen ⟶ Metal Oxide

1) Most <u>metals</u> can react with <u>oxygen</u> to form a <u>metal oxide</u>.

2) The <u>most reactive</u> metals react <u>violently</u> when heated in oxygen, <u>burning</u> with a <u>bright flame</u>.

3) The <u>less reactive</u> metals react <u>more slowly</u> when heated in oxygen.

4) Metals will burn <u>more brightly</u> in <u>pure oxygen</u> than in <u>air</u>, since air is only about <u>21%</u> oxygen.

EXAMPLES:

zinc + oxygen ⟶ zinc oxide

copper + oxygen ⟶ copper oxide

There's more about oxidation reactions on page 57.

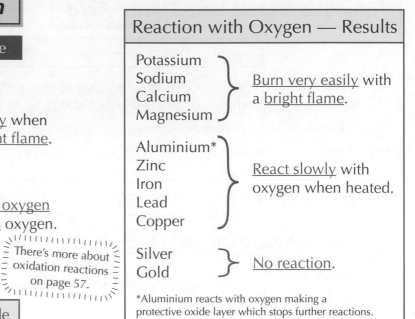

Reaction with Oxygen — Results

Potassium Sodium Calcium Magnesium	<u>Burn very easily</u> with a <u>bright flame</u>.
Aluminium* Zinc Iron Lead Copper	<u>React slowly</u> with oxygen when heated.
Silver Gold	<u>No reaction</u>.

*Aluminium reacts with oxygen making a protective oxide layer which stops further reactions.

Reacting Metals With **Water**

Metal + Water ⟶ Metal Hydroxide + Hydrogen

(or, for less reactive metals:)

Metal + Steam ⟶ Metal Oxide + Hydrogen

1) Metals <u>above</u> hydrogen in the reactivity series will <u>react</u> with <u>water</u> to produce <u>hydrogen</u>.

2) The <u>more</u> reactive metals react vigorously with <u>cold water</u> to produce <u>hydroxides</u>.

3) The <u>less</u> reactive metals will react with <u>steam</u> to make <u>oxides</u>.

4) Metals <u>below</u> hydrogen in the reactivity series <u>won't</u> react with <u>cold water</u> or <u>steam</u>.

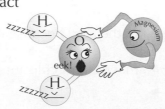

EXAMPLES:

sodium + water ⟶ sodium hydroxide + hydrogen

magnesium + steam ⟶ magnesium oxide + hydrogen

Reaction with Water — Results

Potassium Sodium Calcium	React with <u>cold water</u>.
Magnesium Aluminium* Zinc Iron	React with <u>steam</u>.
Lead Copper Silver Gold	<u>No reaction</u> with water or steam. (Lead does react, but only <u>incredibly</u> slowly.)

*Aluminium reacts with oxygen making a protective oxide layer which stops further reactions.

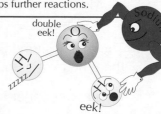

Silver — it reacts with nothing — and rhymes with nothing...

There are two different types of reaction on this page: 1) metals with oxygen 2) metals with water. For each type, the metals split into 3 groups. Learn all those details, then cover and scribble.

Displacement Reactions

This page is pretty crammed, but the stuff on it is actually pretty easy, I promise...

'Displacement' Means 'Taking the Place of'

Learn this rule:

> A more reactive metal will displace a less reactive metal from its compound.

1) The reactivity series (see page 62) tells you which are the most reactive metals — i.e. the ones which react most strongly with other things.

2) If you put a more reactive metal like magnesium into a salt solution of a less reactive metal, like copper sulfate, then magnesium will take the place of the copper — and make magnesium sulfate.

3) The "kicked out" metal then coats itself on the reactive metal, so we'd see copper.

4) This only happens if the metal added is more reactive — higher displaces lower. Got it?

5) You can use this kind of reaction to work out for yourself where metals belong in the reactivity series.

A **Reactivity Series** Investigation

Method: Slap bits of different metals into some salt solutions and see what happens.

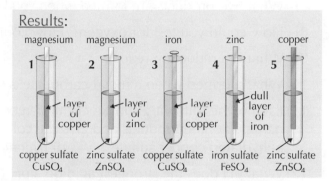

Results:

Tube 1: The blue copper sulfate solution goes colourless and copper coats the magnesium strip.

Magnesium must be more reactive than copper as it takes its place.

magnesium + copper sulfate ⟶ magnesium sulfate + copper

Tube 2: Zinc is seen coating the magnesium strip.
Magnesium must be more reactive than zinc as it takes its place.

magnesium + zinc sulfate ⟶ magnesium sulfate + zinc

Tube 3: The blue copper sulfate solution goes green and copper coats the nail.
Iron must be more reactive than copper as it takes its place.

iron + copper sulfate ⟶ iron sulfate + copper

Tube 4: Iron is seen coating the zinc strip. Zinc must be more reactive than iron as it takes its place.

zinc + iron sulfate ⟶ zinc sulfate + iron

Tube 5: There's no reaction. Copper can't displace zinc — it's not reactive enough.

Most Reactive   Magnesium   Zinc   Iron   Copper   Least Reactive

Metals Can be Displaced from Their Oxides Too

1) As with metal sulfates, a metal can be displaced from its oxide by a more reactive metal.

2) For example, heating a mixture of copper oxide powder (which is black) and powdered magnesium metal (which is grey) forms white magnesium oxide and orange copper metal.

3) Magnesium is more reactive than copper, so it kicks it out of the oxide and takes its place:

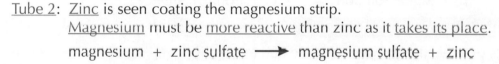

magnesium + copper oxide ⟶ magnesium oxide + copper

Section 7 — Chemical Changes

Summary Questions

There's no use getting through a whole section of Chemistry if you can't summarise it with a handy set of questions that test everything you need to know. You know what to do by now — work through the questions one by one, make sure you know everything, then maybe treat yourself to something sweet.

1) Give two examples of: a) substances made by chemical reactions
                          b) chemical reactions that might happen in your home.

2) What are the three types of flame that a Bunsen burner can produce? Explain what each type of flame is used for, and how you would adjust the Bunsen burner to produce each one.

3) Does the total mass of the reactants and products change in a chemical reaction? Why or why not?

4) What's the name of the process in which a chemical gains oxygen?

5) What is combustion? What three things are needed for combustion?

6) Each of the following substances is burned in oxygen. Give the product(s) for each reaction.
   a) carbon   b) sulfur   c) iron   d) magnesium

7) What two products are formed when you burn methane in oxygen?

8) How could you test for oxygen? How could you test for carbon dioxide?

9) What is a reduction reaction?

10) What's formed when a metal carbonate is broken down by thermal decomposition?

11) Each of the following substances undergoes thermal decomposition. For each reaction, name all of the products and give the colours of the solid reactants and products.
    a) hydrated copper sulfate   b) hydrated cobalt chloride   c) potassium permanganate

12) What pH does the strongest acid on a pH chart have? And the strongest alkali?

13) What colour would Universal indicator go if it was mixed with:
    a) a strong acid   b) a neutral solution   c) a strong alkali?

14) What is neutralisation?

15) What are the products of a reaction between an acid and an alkali?

16) What products are formed when an acid reacts with a metal carbonate?

17) Outline a method you could use to make common salt (sodium chloride).

18) Hydrochloric acid reacts with bases to make <u>chloride</u> salts.
    What kind of salts do you get with sulfuric acid? How about nitric acid?

19) Give three examples of useful neutralisation reactions.

20) List the following metals in order of decreasing reactivity:
    iron, gold, sodium, potassium, zinc, calcium, silver, copper, lead, aluminium, magnesium

21) Carbon can be used to extract iron from its oxide ore. Write a word equation for this reaction.

22) What do metals produce when they react with an acid?

23) Which of these metals would react the most violently with a dilute acid: zinc, calcium, or lead?

24) Describe what happens when zinc is heated in oxygen.

25) Why do metals burn more brightly in pure oxygen than air?

26) What is produced when magnesium reacts with steam?

27) Explain why magnesium can displace copper from copper sulfate.

28) What will happen when a mixture of copper oxide and zinc is heated?

The Air

Ah, a brand new section — what a breath of fresh air...

The **Atmosphere** is Mostly **Nitrogen** and **Oxygen**

1) The <u>gases</u> that surround a planet make up that planet's <u>atmosphere</u>.
2) The <u>Earth's atmosphere</u> is around:

    78% nitrogen (N_2)   21% oxygen (O_2)   0.04% carbon dioxide (CO_2)

It also contains <u>small amounts</u> of other gases, like <u>argon</u> and <u>water vapour</u> (see below).

Investigating the **Proportion** of **Oxygen** in the **Air**

You can do an <u>experiment</u> with <u>iron</u> to show that the atmosphere is around <u>20% oxygen</u>.
Iron reacts with oxygen in the air to form <u>rust</u> (see page 62)
— so iron will <u>remove oxygen</u> from the air. Here's how you do it:

1) First soak some <u>iron wool</u> in <u>water</u> (this speeds up the reaction).
2) Then push the wool into a <u>test tube</u>, put your thumb over the end and put the tube <u>upside down</u> in a beaker of water. Remove your thumb and mark the <u>starting position</u> of the water on the test tube.
3) Over time, the level of the water in the test tube will <u>rise</u>. This is because the iron <u>reacts</u> with the <u>oxygen</u> in the air to make iron oxide (rust). The water rises to <u>fill the space</u> the oxygen took up.
4) About a week later, once the reaction has stopped, mark the <u>finishing position</u> of the water.
5) Remove the test tube from the beaker. <u>Fill the tube</u> with water up to each mark and pour the contents into a <u>measuring cylinder</u> to find out the volume of air in the tube at the <u>start</u> and the <u>end</u>.
6) Use the <u>difference</u> between the start and end volumes to work out the percentage of the <u>starting volume</u> that has been used up — it should be about 20%.

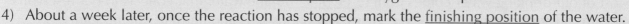

(Diagram labels: Iron wool, Finishing position of water, Starting position of water, Water)

The **Atmosphere** Also Contains **Water Vapour**

1) The amount of <u>water vapour</u> in the air can <u>vary</u> quite a lot (from nearly 0% to about 4%), depending on where you are.
2) You can <u>test</u> for water vapour in the air with <u>anhydrous copper sulfate</u> or <u>anhydrous cobalt chloride</u>:

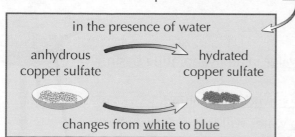

in the presence of water
anhydrous copper sulfate → hydrated copper sulfate
changes from <u>white</u> to <u>blue</u>

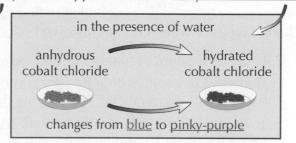

in the presence of water
anhydrous cobalt chloride → hydrated cobalt chloride
changes from <u>blue</u> to <u>pinky-purple</u>

Nitrogen is in the air — doo do doo, doo do doo....

Make sure you know the proportions of each of the different gases found in the atmosphere. You need to learn the three experiments on this page too. The eagle-eyed amongst you might have also spotted that the tests for water vapour are the reverse of the thermal decomposition reactions on page 58.

Water

This page is swimming in watery goodness. Grab your snorkel and let's dive in...

The **Water Cycle** Involves **Evaporation** and **Condensation**

1) Water is found in <u>abundance</u> on <u>Earth</u> — this means there's a lot of it about.

2) The water on Earth is constantly being <u>recycled</u> in the <u>water cycle</u>:

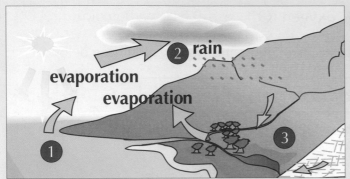

1 Heat from the <u>Sun</u> makes water from the seas, lakes and rivers <u>evaporate</u> into <u>water vapour</u>. (<u>Clouds</u> are water vapour — tiny droplets of water hanging around in the air.)

2 As the water vapour <u>rises</u>, it <u>cools</u> and <u>condenses</u> and falls as <u>rain</u> (hail or snow if it's really cold).

3 The water <u>flows back</u> to the sea in <u>rivers</u> and <u>glaciers</u>.

3) The amount of water that evaporates is affected by <u>temperature</u> and <u>air flow</u> — <u>high temperatures</u> and <u>strong winds</u> cause <u>more water</u> to evaporate from seas, lakes and rivers.

4) If you've carried out lab <u>experiments</u> involving <u>evaporation</u>, you might have seen a similar thing — water is lost <u>more quickly</u> in a <u>warm, drafty room</u> than in a <u>cold, still room</u>.

Drinking Water Needs to be Good Quality

1) Most of our drinking water comes from <u>reservoirs</u>. But the water that collects in our reservoirs contains all sorts of <u>nasty stuff</u> — e.g. twigs, <u>poisonous salts</u> and <u>harmful microorganisms</u>.

2) Thankfully these things are <u>filtered out</u> in <u>water treatment plants</u> before the water comes out of our taps. This helps to <u>stop</u> the water we drink <u>making us ill</u>.

Distilled Water is Pure Water

1) <u>Sea water</u> is far from pure. It contains <u>sodium chloride</u> (table salt) and other <u>salts</u>.

2) <u>Tap water</u> still contains some <u>dissolved salts</u> — some soluble impurities in the water <u>can't</u> be <u>filtered out</u> in water treatment plants. To make pure water you need to <u>remove all the salts</u>.

3) <u>Totally pure water</u> with <u>nothing</u> dissolved in it can be produced by <u>distillation</u> — <u>boiling</u> water to make steam and <u>condensing</u> the steam (see page 49).

evaporating water

salts

4) You can carry out a simple <u>experiment</u> to find out if different types of water contain <u>dissolved salts</u>:

1) Put a small amount of <u>sea</u>, <u>tap</u> or <u>distilled water</u> in an <u>evaporating basin</u>.
2) Heat the water gently with a <u>Bunsen burner</u>. The water will <u>evaporate</u> off, leaving any <u>dissolved salts</u> behind.
3) <u>Sea</u> water will leave <u>lots of salts</u> behind, <u>tap</u> water will leave <u>some salts</u> but <u>distilled</u> water should leave <u>no</u> salts at all.

You've had a read of this page — now let's test the water...

Start off memorising the headings — when you've done that, cover the page and write them down. Then try a mini-essay for each one to see what else you've learnt. Then look back and learn some more.

The Effects of Fossil Fuels

We burn a lot of fossil fuels these days — unfortunately this makes a bit of a mess of the environment...

Burning Fossil Fuels Releases Gases and Particles

1) We burn huge amounts of fossil fuels (oil, coal and gas) to make electricity — see page 106. Cars also burn lots of fossil fuel (petrol and diesel are made from oil).

2) Fossil fuels are hydrocarbons — they contain carbon and hydrogen. During the combustion of fossil fuels carbon dioxide and water vapour are released into the atmosphere. Energy (as heat and light) is also produced.

> hydrocarbon + oxygen ⟶ carbon dioxide + water vapour (+ energy)

3) If there's not enough oxygen, some of the fuel doesn't burn, and solid particles (called particulates) of soot (carbon) and unburnt fuel are released. Carbon monoxide (a poisonous gas) is also released.

Sulfur Dioxide Causes Acid Rain

1) If a fuel contains sulfur impurities, the sulfur will be released as sulfur dioxide when the fuel is burnt.

2) When the sulfur dioxide mixes with clouds it forms dilute sulfuric acid. This then falls as acid rain.

3) Acid rain can cause plants and animals to die and can also damage buildings (see page 71).

You can Reduce Acid Rain by Reducing Sulfur Emissions

1) Sulfur can be removed from fuels before they're burnt, or afterwards from the waste gases.

2) For example, sulfur is removed from petrol and diesel before it is used in vehicles, and gas scrubbers are used in power stations to remove sulfur from the waste gases after combustion.

3) The other way of reducing acid rain is simply to reduce our usage of fossil fuels.

Increasing Carbon Dioxide Causes Climate Change

1) Carbon dioxide is what's known as a greenhouse gas. This means it traps heat from the Sun in the Earth's atmosphere. This stops some heat from being lost into space and helps to keep the Earth warm.

2) But burning fossil fuels increases the level of carbon dioxide in the atmosphere — and so the Earth is gradually getting hotter.

3) This increase in the Earth's temperature is called global warming.

4) Global warming is a type of climate change. It could have some serious effects — e.g. flooding in coastal areas due to the polar ice caps melting, a change in rainfall patterns which might make it harder for farmers to grow crops.

We Need to Reduce Carbon Dioxide Levels

1) The most obvious thing we can do is to reduce the amount of fossil fuels we burn.

2) We can also reduce deforestation and plant more trees. Trees use carbon dioxide for photosynthesis (see page 24), so more trees means more carbon dioxide is removed from the atmosphere.

Limestone

Limestone's often formed from sea shells, so you might not expect that it'd be a great building material...

Limestone is Mainly **Calcium Carbonate**

Limestone is mainly <u>calcium carbonate</u> ($CaCO_3$), and is quarried out of the ground. It has lots of different uses in <u>construction</u>:

St Paul's Cathedral is made from limestone.

1) It's great for making into <u>blocks</u> for building with. Fine old buildings like <u>cathedrals</u> are often made purely from limestone blocks.

2) Limestone is used in the <u>manufacture</u> of <u>cement</u>, <u>mortar</u>, <u>concrete</u> and <u>glass</u>, as well as in the extraction of <u>iron</u> from iron ore.

3) It is also heated to <u>produce quicklime</u> (calcium oxide), which can be used as a building material.

Limestone Reacts with **Acids**

1) Even though limestone is pretty sturdy stuff, don't go thinking it doesn't react with anything.

2) Limestone reacts with <u>acids</u> in the same way as other <u>metal carbonates</u> (see page 60). For example, limestone reacts with <u>dilute hydrochloric acid</u> to make a <u>salt</u>, <u>water</u> and <u>carbon dioxide</u>.

> calcium carbonate + hydrochloric acid $\longrightarrow$ calcium chloride + water + carbon dioxide

3) Unfortunately the reaction between <u>calcium carbonate</u> and <u>acids</u> means that limestone buildings can be <u>damaged</u> by <u>acid rain</u> (there's more about this on the next page).

Limestone can be **Thermally Decomposed**

1) <u>Thermal decomposition</u> is when one substance <u>chemically changes</u> into at least two <u>new</u> substances when it's <u>heated</u>.

2) When calcium carbonate is heated it <u>thermally decomposes</u> to make <u>calcium oxide</u> and <u>carbon dioxide</u>.

> calcium carbonate $\longrightarrow$ calcium oxide + carbon dioxide

3) The <u>calcium oxide</u> can be really useful for <u>farmers</u> (see below).

There's loads more about thermal decomposition on page 58.

Limestone is Also Used in **Agriculture**

1) When you <u>add water</u> to calcium oxide you get <u>calcium hydroxide</u> (also called <u>slaked lime</u>).

> calcium oxide + water $\longrightarrow$ calcium hydroxide

2) Calcium hydroxide is an <u>alkali</u> which can be used to neutralise <u>acidic soil</u> in fields. Powdered limestone and calcium oxide can be used for this too, but the <u>advantage</u> of <u>calcium hydroxide</u> is that it works <u>much faster</u>.

Limestone — high in Vitamin C-shells...

Don't give me that stony glare. That joke was sublime. Okay fine, I'll stop, there's no need to look so mortar-fied. Right, now it's lime — whoops, time — to get cracking with the learning. Practise writing out the page until it's cemented in your brain. Sorry, I'm done now. I've had my time in the limelight.

Acids in the Environment

You briefly met acid rain a couple of pages ago. But there's still a fair bit more to learn...

Rain *is* Naturally Acidic

1) Rain is naturally a bit acidic due to carbon dioxide in the air.
2) Carbon dioxide dissolves in rain water to make carbonic acid.
3) Gases such as sulfur dioxide in the atmosphere make rain even more acidic and create 'acid rain' (see page 69).

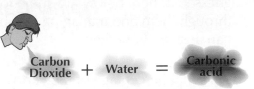

Carbon Dioxide + Water = Carbonic acid

Acids *Attack* Metals

1) When metals above hydrogen in the reactivity series are exposed to acids, they corrode by chemical reaction.
2) The metal reacts with the acid to produce a salt and hydrogen:

$$\text{metal} + \text{acid} \longrightarrow \text{salt} + \text{hydrogen}$$

3) This weakens the metal with devastating effects. For example, acid rain attacks exposed metals in statues and bridges.
4) Things made out of metals lower down the reactivity series are likely to be least affected.

Bad Idea

Better Idea

MAGNESIUM STATUE   BRONZE STATUE

Acid Rain *can* Eat Away *at* Limestone

1) Rocks like limestone, chalk and marble contain calcium carbonate.
2) If acid rain falls onto these rocks a chemical reaction turns them into a calcium salt, water and carbon dioxide.
3) This material is then washed away, damaging the rock. When rocks gradually wear away like this it's called chemical weathering.
4) The natural acidity in rainwater slowly hollows out caves in limestone rock and eats away at limestone cliffs.
5) Acid rain speeds up this weathering process.
6) Buildings and statues made of limestone are also damaged by acid rain.

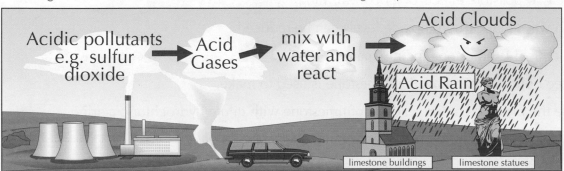

Acid Clouds

Acidic pollutants e.g. sulfur dioxide → Acid Gases → mix with water and react → Acid Rain

limestone buildings   limestone statues

I'm singing in the acid rain, just singing in the acid rain...

This page has three sections — each one has a heading, several numbered points and a smattering of pictures. Learn them bit by bit. Keep testing how much you've learnt by covering the page and scribbling down what you've learnt. Once you've memorised everything, go and put your feet up.

Summary Questions

Well there we are. The end of Section 8. All you have to do now is learn it all. And yes you've guessed it, here below are some lovely questions I prepared earlier. It's no good just idly going through them and managing half-baked answers to one or two that take your fancy. Make sure you can answer all of them.

1) What percentage of the Earth's atmosphere is: a) nitrogen, b) oxygen, c) carbon dioxide?

2) Name one other gas present in the Earth's atmosphere in tiny amounts.

3) Describe an experiment you could do to estimate the proportion of oxygen in the atmosphere.

4) Give two substances you could use to test for water vapour in the air.
Describe how each substance changes colour in the presence of water vapour.

5) Give a brief description of the water cycle.

6) a) Describe how wind affects the amount of water that evaporates from a lake.
b) During a lab experiment, would you expect water to evaporate more quickly
   in a warm room or in a cold room?

7) How are harmful substances removed from our drinking water in a water treatment plant?
Why is this important?

8) What process is used to produce pure water?

9) Does tap water contain more or less dissolved salts than sea water?

10) Give two human activities that burn lots of fossil fuels.

11) Name three things that can be released during the
combustion of fossil fuels if there's not enough oxygen.

12) If a fuel contains sulfur impurities, what will be released when the fuel is burnt?

13) What acid is formed when sulfur dioxide mixes with clouds?

14) Give two ways that sulfur emissions can be reduced.

15) How does carbon dioxide help to keep the Earth warm?

16) What is global warming? What's causing it?

17) Describe two possible effects of global warming.

18) Give two ways that carbon dioxide levels can be reduced.

19) What chemical is limestone mainly made up of?

20) Give three building materials that limestone is used to make.

21) What are the products of the reaction of limestone with dilute hydrochloric acid?

22) What two substances are produced if calcium carbonate is heated?

23) How is limestone used in agriculture?

24) Explain why rain is naturally acidic.

25) Explain how acid rain may damage a metal bridge.

26) Explain why acid rain is a problem for limestone buildings and statues.

Section 8 — The Atmosphere

Electrical Circuits

First up in this section, a page that covers all the really basic stuff about electricity...

Electric Current is the Flow of Charge

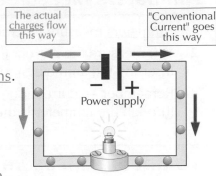

1) Electric current is the flow of charge around a circuit.
2) It can only flow if a circuit is complete.
3) The moving charges are negatively charged particles called electrons.
4) Irritatingly, they flow the opposite way to the direction of conventional current, which is shown on circuits as arrows pointing always from positive to negative.
5) It's vital that you realise that current is not used up as it flows through a circuit. The total current in the circuit is always the same.

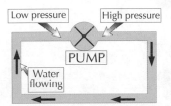

Current is a bit like water flowing...

The pump drives the water along like a power supply. The water is there at the pump and is still there when it returns to it — and just like the water, electric current in a circuit doesn't get used up either.

Voltage Pushes the Current Around

1) In a circuit the battery acts like a pump — it provides the driving force to push the charge round the circuit. This driving force is called the voltage.

Voltage is sometimes called potential difference.

2) If you increase the voltage more current will flow.
3) Different batteries have different voltages. Putting several batteries together makes a bigger voltage.

Resistance is How Easily Electricity Can Flow

1) Resistance is anything in a circuit that slows down the flow of current.
2) The lower the resistance of a component, the better it is at conducting electricity.

A component is anything you put in a circuit.

3) So as long as the voltage stays the same, the lower the resistance of a component, the greater the current through it.
4) The number of components in a circuit affects the current too — more components increase the resistance and slow down the current.
5) Components and materials that electricity can easily travel through (e.g. metals) are called conductors — they have low resistance.
6) Insulators (e.g. wood) are components and materials that don't easily allow electric charges to pass through them — they have high resistance.

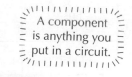

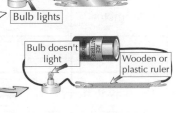

Batteries Transfer Energy to Other Components

1) Batteries store chemical energy (see page 102).
2) This chemical energy is transformed into electrical energy, which flows round the circuit.
3) The electrical energy is transferred to the components and is transformed into different kinds of energy, e.g. bulbs transform electrical energy into light energy.

More on Electrical Circuits

You don't just need to know what current and voltage are — you need to be able to measure them too.

Ammeters Measure Current

1) <u>Ammeters</u> measure electric <u>current</u>. It's measured in <u>amperes</u> (or amps, A, for short).

2) You measure the current <u>through</u> a circuit by inserting the ammeter <u>into</u> the circuit like this:

3) Remember — current <u>doesn't</u> get used up, so the current through the ammeter is the <u>same</u> as through the bulb.

Voltmeters Measure Voltage

1) <u>Voltmeters</u> measure <u>voltage</u> in <u>volts</u> (or V for short).

2) You measure the voltage <u>across</u> something in the circuit, such as a bulb.

3) To measure the voltage across a bulb, you'd connect a <u>voltmeter across</u> it like this:

Lots of Components can be Put in Circuits

You've probably already come across <u>circuit diagrams</u> — simplified diagrams of <u>real circuits</u> showing all the <u>components</u> as <u>symbols</u>. Well, here are some more <u>components</u> you need to know about and their <u>symbols</u>:

Make sure you know how to draw component symbols the right way round in a circuit diagram. In all the symbols here, current is flowing left to right.

Component	Symbol	Description
Battery		Power source
Fuse		Breaks the circuit if current is too high
Resistor		Reduces current
Variable Resistor		Gives control over reduction in current
Ammeter	(A)	Measures current
SPST		Simple on-off switch
Reed Switch		Switch controlled by a magnetic field
Electromagnet		Coil of wire with magnetic field

Component	Symbol	Description
Push-button Switch		Switch controlled by button
Light Emitting Diode (LED)		Lights up when a current is passed through
Light Dependent Resistor (LDR)		Resistance decreases when light is shone on it
Semiconductor Diode		Only lets current flow in one direction
Relay		Switch controlled by an electromagnet
Junction of Conductors		Point where current has a choice of multiple paths

A kilogram of bacon? — Weigh it on the 'ammeter...

Ammeters measure current and voltmeters measure voltage — easy enough. Remembering all those components is a bit tricker. Who wouldn't want to be able to draw loads of circuit diagrams though?

Series and Parallel Circuits

The big difference between series and parallel circuits is that in parallel circuits, current can take different routes around the circuit. And the charges don't even need a map or a GPS to do it...

Series Circuits — *Current has No Choice of Route*

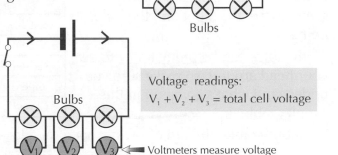

1) In the circuit on the right current flows out of the <u>cell</u>, through the <u>ammeter</u>, the <u>bulbs</u>, then through the other ammeter and the <u>switch</u> and back to the <u>cell</u>. As it passes through, the current gives up some of its <u>energy</u> to the bulbs.

> A cell is a single electrical energy source.
> A battery is two or more cells put together.

Ammeters measure current

Ammeter readings: $A_1 = A_2$

Bulbs

2) The current is the <u>same anywhere</u> in this circuit as the current has no choice of route. Did I tell you <u>current isn't used up</u> — well don't forget.

> In series circuits the current is either on or off — the switch being open or any other break in the circuit will stop the current flowing everywhere.

3) In series circuits, the <u>voltages</u> across the components <u>add up</u> to the voltage of the cell (or battery).

Bulbs

Voltage readings: $V_1 + V_2 + V_3$ = total cell voltage

Voltmeters measure voltage

Parallel Circuits — *Current has a Choice*

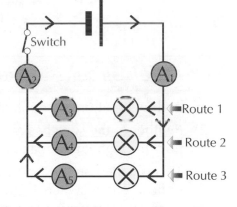

1) In the circuit shown, current flows <u>out</u> of the <u>cell</u> and it <u>all</u> flows through the first ammeter A_1. It then has a "choice" of <u>three</u> routes and the current <u>splits</u> down routes <u>1</u>, <u>2</u> and <u>3</u>.

Switch

Route 1
Route 2
Route 3

2) The readings of ammeters A_3, A_4 and A_5 will usually be <u>different</u>, depending on the <u>resistances</u> of the components — i.e. the bulbs.

3) The three currents <u>join up</u> again on their way back to the cell. So the readings of $A_3 + A_4 + A_5$ added together will be equal to the reading for current on ammeter A_2 (which will <u>also</u> equal A_1).

4) It's difficult to believe I know, but the current through A_1 is the <u>same</u> as the current through A_2 — the current is <u>not used up</u>. (I may have told you that once or twice already.)

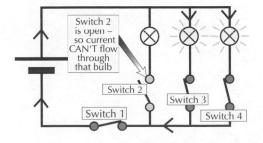

Switch 2 is open – so current CAN'T flow through that bulb

Switch 2
Switch 3
Switch 1
Switch 4

5) Parallel circuits are <u>sensible</u> because part of them can be <u>on</u> while other bits are <u>off</u>. In the circuit here, <u>two</u> bulbs are <u>on</u> and the other one is <u>off</u>.

6) Don't get confused — the <u>voltage</u> across each bulb in this circuit is <u>equal to</u> the voltage of the cell.

A series of circuits — well, there are four on this page...

Circuits cause people a lot of gyp, that's for sure. The worst thing about them is that you can't actually see the current flowing, so it's very difficult to appreciate what's going on. Toughsky.

AND and OR Circuits

Putting switches into circuits lets us do some very clever things. Prepare to be amazed...

Series Circuits Make '**AND**' Circuits

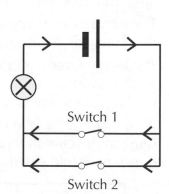

1) In the circuit on the right, the current will only flow, and the bulb will only come on, when <u>both switches</u> are closed.

2) If one or both of the switches are open, there will be a <u>break in the circuit</u>.

3) This is an <u>'AND' circuit</u> because for the current to flow, switch 1 <u>AND</u> switch 2 have to be closed.

'**AND**' Circuit **Truth Table**

1) A truth table links a set of <u>inputs</u> to an <u>output</u>.

2) In this case, the status of the two <u>switches</u> are the <u>input</u> and the <u>bulb</u> being on or off is the <u>output</u>.

3) Truth tables can be <u>pretty tricky</u> to get your head around, so make sure you understand what's going on in this simpler table first:

Input		Output
Switch 1	Switch 2	Bulb
Open	Open	Open
Closed	Open	Open
Open	Closed	Open
Closed	Closed	Closed

Remember, the bulb only comes on when Switch 1 AND Switch 2 are closed.

4) For a truth table, instead of saying '<u>open</u>' or '<u>closed</u>', you'll need to use '<u>true</u>' or '<u>false</u>'.

5) Ask yourself if there's a <u>current flowing</u> through the <u>component</u>.

6) If the answer is <u>yes</u>, write <u>T</u> (true). If the answer is <u>no</u>, write <u>F</u> (false).

7) So the truth table for the circuit at the top of the page looks like this:

Input		Output
Switch 1	Switch 2	Bulb
F	F	F
T	F	F
F	T	F
T	T	T

Just to add a bit more confusion to the mix, sometimes '1' is used instead of 'T' and '0' is used instead of 'F'.

Parallel Circuits Make '**OR**' Circuits

1) In the circuit on the right, the current has <u>two paths</u> to flow through.

2) If <u>either of the switches</u> are closed, current will flow through it and make the bulb come on.

3) This is called an <u>'OR' circuit</u> because for the current to flow, either switch 1 <u>OR</u> switch 2 has to be closed.

'**OR**' Circuit **Truth Table**

The truth table for the circuit here looks like this:

Input		Output
Switch 1	Switch 2	Bulb
F	F	F
T	F	T
F	T	T
T	T	T

Remember, the bulb will only be off (F) if both switches are open (F).

To tell you the truth, I love tables...

This stuff can be a little bit tricky to wrap your noggin around at first. Just make sure you understand how series and parallel circuits work and how to write a truth table — you'll be laughing in the exam.

Magnets

Magnets can push and pull each other without touching. Sounds like magic, right? Nah, it's just science.

Magnets *are* Surrounded *by* Fields

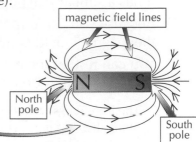

magnetic field lines

North pole

South pole

1) Bar magnets are (surprisingly enough) magnets that are in the shape of a bar. One end of the bar magnet is called the North pole (or North-seeking pole) and the other end is called the South pole (or South-seeking pole).

2) All bar magnets have invisible magnetic fields round them.

3) A magnetic field is a region where magnetic materials (e.g. iron) experience a force.

4) You can draw a magnetic field using lines called magnetic field lines. The magnetic field lines always point from the N-pole to the S-pole.

5) This is what the magnetic field around a bar magnet looks like:

Opposite Poles *Attract* — *Like* Poles *Repel*

Magnets don't need to touch for there to be a force between them.

Attraction

North poles and South poles are attracted to each other.

Repulsion

If you try and bring two of the same type of magnetic pole together, they repel each other.

The only way to check whether a material is a magnet, is to hold it next to a known magnet to test for repulsion.

Iron *Will be* Attracted *to a* North *or* South Pole

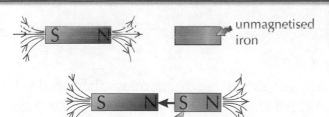

unmagnetised iron

iron becomes magnetised

1) Normally, iron isn't a magnet — we call this unmagnetised iron.

2) But it starts to behave like a magnet, with a magnetic field around it, when it comes close to a magnet.

3) Iron will be attracted to any magnetic pole it is close to — either North or South.

The Earth *has a* Magnetic Field

1) The Earth has a magnetic field. It has a North pole and a South pole, just like a bar magnet.

2) A freely suspended (hanging) bar magnet will always align itself north-south in line with the Earth's magnetic field (unless it's really close to another magnet).

Magnets are like farmers — surrounded by fields...

Magnets are fab aren't they? All that pulling and pushing without even touching. Make sure you know all the fun magnetic facts here. You know the drill by now — learn, cover and scribble.

Electromagnets

Bar magnets stay magnetic all the time. Electromagnets are fancy magnets which you can turn on and off.

A *Wire* With a *Current in it* Has a *Magnetic Field* Round it

1) An electromagnet is made from a coil of insulated wire with a current passing through it.

2) When current runs through the coil of wire,
    it has a similar magnetic field pattern to a bar magnet.

3) Because you can turn the current on and off,
    the magnetic field can be turned on and off.

4) You can test for the magnetic field of an electromagnet
    using iron filings or a plotting compass...

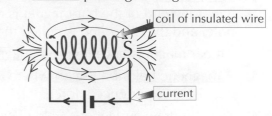

The iron filings will align
along the field lines which
looks quite jolly.

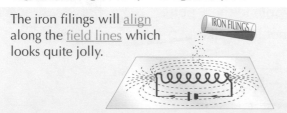

The plotting compass will
always point from N to S
along the field lines wherever
it's placed in the field.
The field lines always point
from North to South.

You Can *Increase* the *Strength* of an *Electromagnet*

1) More current
    in the wire.

2) More turns on
    the coil.

3) A core of soft iron
    inside the coil.

You can't just use any metal to make
an electromagnet core. Soft iron has
to be used for the core to make it
perform as an electromagnet should
— i.e. turning on and off when the
current is turned on and off.

You can make an electromagnet by coiling
some insulated wire round an iron nail and then
connecting the ends of the wire to a battery.

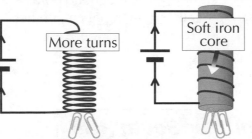

Electromagnets are Really *Useful*

1) Electromagnets can be used in lots of different ways.

2) For example, the lifting magnets used to lift metal in scrap yards are electromagnets. They need to be
    electromagnets so that the 'magnet' effect can be switched off — or else they'd never drop the metal.

Electromagnets Are also *Used in Relays*

1) Relays link together two circuits, so that turning on one circuit causes the other to turn on too.

2) They are used to turn on very high-current circuits using a lower-current circuit,
    as they help to stop the user from coming into contact with the high current.

Example — a shower

1) When the small current is switched on the
    electromagnet activates and the iron lever is
    attracted to it. This makes the lever rotate.

2) As it rotates the other end of the lever pushes
    the contacts together which turns on the
    other circuit and makes the shower work.

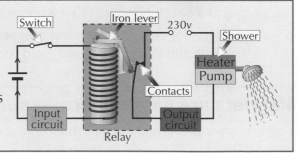

Summary Questions

Phew. Electricity and Magnetism — it's no holiday, that's for sure. There are certainly quite a few grisly bits and bobs in this section. But life isn't all bad — just look at all these lovely questions I've cooked up for your enjoyment. They're in the same order as the stuff appears throughout Section 9 — so for any you can't do, just look back, find the answer, and then learn it good and proper for next time.

1) Current is the flow of what?

2) Can current flow in an incomplete circuit?

3) What job does a battery do in a circuit?

4) What is voltage?

5) What is resistance?

6) What is the difference between a conductor and an insulator?

7) What kind of energy transfer takes place from a battery to a circuit?

8) What instrument do we use to measure current? How would you connect it in a circuit?

9) What are the units of current?

10) What instrument do we use to measure voltage? How would you connect it in a circuit?

11) What are the units of voltage?

12) Sketch the symbol for all of these components:
   a) a battery   b) a resistor   c) an ammeter
   d) an SPST (open)   e) a light emitting diode   f) a relay.

13) Describe what a semiconductor diode is. Draw its symbol.

14)* A series circuit contains 3 bulbs. A current of 3 A flows through the first bulb. What current flows through the third bulb?

15) What happens if there is a break in a series circuit?

16) Which type of circuit allows part of the circuit to be switched off?

17) In parallel circuits current has a choice of what?

18) True or false? Adding the current through each branch of a parallel circuit gives you the total current.

19) Draw an AND circuit with two switches and an LED and write out a truth table for it.

20) Write out a truth table for the circuit on the right.

21) What is a magnetic field? In which direction do field lines always go?

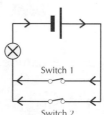

22) Name two magnetic poles that will: a) attract each other   b) repel each other.

23) Explain what will happen when unmagnetised iron is put next to the North pole of a bar magnet.

24) What's an electromagnet?

25) Sketch a diagram showing how a plotting compass points around an electromagnet.

26) List three ways to increase the strength of an electromagnet.

27) Explain why electromagnets are useful in scrapyards.

28) What is a relay?

29) Describe how a relay is used in a shower circuit.

---

* Answer on page 116.   *Section 9 — Electricity and Magnetism*

Speed

Neeeoww... Yes, it's a page on speed. Make sure you can do these calculations. Don't zoom through.

*Speed is **How Fast** You're **Going***

1) <u>Speed</u> is a <u>measure</u> of how <u>far</u> you travel in a <u>set</u> amount of <u>time</u>.

2) The <u>formula triangle</u> is definitely the <u>best</u> way to do <u>speed calculations</u>.

$$\text{Speed} = \frac{\text{Distance}}{\text{Time}}$$

This line means divided by or shared by (÷).

A formula triangle

3) Use the word <u>SIDOT</u> to help you remember the formula:

<u>SIDOT</u> — <u>S</u>peed <u>I</u>s <u>D</u>istance <u>O</u>ver <u>T</u>ime.

<u>Always</u> use <u>UNITS</u>.

4) There are <u>three</u> common <u>units</u> for speed. ⟹ You can see that they're all kind of the same, i.e. <u>distance unit</u> per <u>time unit</u>.

<u>metres</u> per <u>second</u> — m/s
<u>miles</u> per <u>hour</u> — mph or miles/h
<u>kilometres</u> per <u>hour</u> — km/h

*Work Out **Speed** Using **Distance** and **Time***

To work out <u>speed</u> you need to know the <u>distance travelled</u> and the <u>time taken</u>.

<u>EXAMPLE 1</u>: A boy is skateboarding down a path. You notice it takes exactly <u>5 seconds</u> to move between two fence posts, <u>10 metres</u> apart. <u>What's the boy's speed?</u>

10m

ANSWER 1:   <u>Step 1)</u>   <u>Write down what you know</u>:
distance, d = 10 m   time, t = 5 s

<u>Step 2)</u>   <u>We want to find speed</u>, s from the formula triangle: s = d/t
Speed = Distance ÷ Time   = 10 ÷ 5   = <u>2 m/s</u>

Put your finger over "s" in the formula triangle — which leaves d/t (i.e. d ÷ t).

Speed questions are a <u>doddle</u> if you just learn the <u>formula triangle</u>.

<u>EXAMPLE 2</u>: A campervan travels 15 miles in 30 minutes. <u>What's its speed?</u>

ANSWER 2:   <u>Step 1)</u>   <u>Write down what you know</u>:
distance, d = 15 miles   time, t = 30 minutes = 0.5 of an hour.

<u>Step 2)</u>   <u>We want to find speed</u>, s, from the formula triangle: s = d/t
Speed = Distance ÷ Time   = 15 ÷ 0.5   = <u>30 miles/hour</u> (mph)

For the <u>answer</u> to be in <u>miles per hour</u> you need the <u>distance</u> in <u>miles</u> and the <u>time</u> in <u>hours</u> so the 30 mins had to become 0.5 hrs.

Speed is ace — well it takes some beating...

Speed is a pretty simple idea really. This page has all the basic and important facts about speed. There's the formula for a start, the units, and then a couple of worked examples. Learn it all. Now.

Forces and Movement

Well, I can't force you to read this page — but if I were you, I'd push on with it...

Forces are Nearly Always Pushes and Pulls

1) Forces are pushes or pulls that occur when two objects interact.
2) Forces can't be seen, but the effects of a force can be seen.
3) Forces are measured in newtons — N.
4) They usually act in pairs.
5) They always act in a certain direction.
6) A newton meter is used to measure forces.
7) Objects don't need to touch to interact. For example, forces between magnets (page 77).

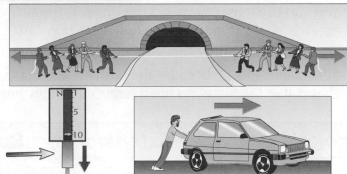

Forces Can Make Objects Do Five Things

1. Speed Up or Start Moving	Like kicking a football. To start something moving, a push force must be larger than resisting forces like friction (see page 83).	3. Change Direction	Like hitting a ball with a bat or gravity causing footballs to come back down to Earth.
		4. Turn	Like turning a spanner.
2. Slow Down or Stop Moving	Like drag (air resistance) or friction (see page 83).	5. Change Shape	Like stretching and compressing (see p. 82), bending and twisting. Changing shape — Stretching, Bending, Compressing, Twisting

Learn These Two Important Statements

Balanced Forces produce No Change in Movement

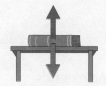

Gravity acting on the book is balanced by the upward force of the table.

Peddling force is balanced by drag and friction from the road, so the cyclist moves at a constant speed.

Unbalanced Forces Change the Speed and/or Direction of Objects

The upward lift force is greater than the downwards force of the child, so the lid moves upwards.

The force from the boat's motor is greater than the resistance from the water, so the boat speeds up.

Force is ace — well it beats speed...

Luckily there isn't much to learn here — just make sure you do. Learn, cover, scribble, check...

Springs

It's not just about turning, pushing and pulling — forces are also able to stretch or squash things.

*You Can **Deform** Objects by **Stretching** or **Squashing***

1) You can use forces to <u>stretch</u> or <u>compress</u> (squash) objects, e.g. when you stomp on an empty fizzy pop can.

2) The force you apply causes the object to <u>deform</u> (change its shape).

3) <u>Springs</u> are <u>special</u> because they usually <u>spring back</u> into their <u>original shape</u> after the force has been <u>removed</u> — they are <u>elastic</u>.

When something is stretched tight, the force acting is called <u>tension</u>.

*Hooke's Law Says **Extension** of a **Spring** Depends on the **Force***

If a spring is supported at the top and then a weight is attached to the bottom, it <u>stretches</u>.

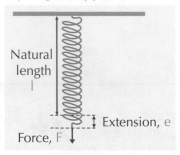

Natural length | l

Extension, e

Force, F

1) <u>Hooke's Law</u> says the amount it stretches (the <u>extension</u>, <u>e</u>), is <u>directly proportional</u> to the <u>force applied</u>, <u>F</u> — i.e. the relationship between force and extension is <u>linear</u>.

2) Some objects <u>obey</u> Hooke's Law, e.g. <u>springs</u>. But it <u>only</u> applies up to a <u>certain force</u>.

k is the <u>spring constant</u>. Its value depends on the material that you're stretching and it's measured in newtons per metre (N/m).

$$\text{Hooke's Law: } F = k \times e$$

*You Can **Investigate** the **Stretching** of a **Spring***

You can <u>investigate Hooke's Law</u> by adding different weights to a spring and recording the <u>extension</u> after each weight:

1) First set up the equipment as in the diagram.

2) Record the position of the <u>bottom of the spring</u>, first <u>without the weight</u> and then <u>with the weight attached</u>.

3) The <u>difference</u> between the two positions is the extension.

extension = position with weight − position without weight

4) Repeat the measurement with <u>different-sized weights</u>.

5) Record your results in a <u>table</u> and plot a <u>graph</u> of <u>weight</u> versus <u>extension</u>.

ruler with cm scale

clamp stand

spring

weight

W

0
2
4
6
8
10
12
14
16
18
20

*Springs Can be Used in **Combination***

You can use springs <u>together</u>. They'll act <u>differently</u> depending on whether they're in <u>series</u> or in <u>parallel</u>.

<u>Springs in series:</u>

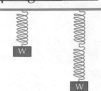

Each spring extends the <u>same amount</u> as an individual spring would, so <u>total extension</u> = extension of one spring × number of springs.

<u>Springs in parallel:</u>

Each spring extends <u>half as much</u> as a single spring, so <u>total extension</u> = extension of one spring ÷ number of springs.

This page will stretch you — better do some extra work on it...

Phew. There's lots to learn here, so cover up the page and try and scribble it ALL down from memory.

Friction and Resistance

It's friction and resistance which mean cars and bikes can slow down. Vive la resistance.

Friction Tries to *Stop Objects Sliding Past* Each Other

Friction is a <u>force</u> that always acts in the <u>opposite</u> direction to movement. It's the force you need to <u>overcome</u> when <u>pushing an object</u> out of the way.

The *Good Points* of Friction — It Allows Things to *Start and Stop*

1) Friction allows the tyres on a bike to <u>grip</u> the road <u>surface</u> — without this grip you couldn't make the bike move <u>forward</u> and you wouldn't be able to <u>stop</u> it either — it'd be like riding on <u>ice</u>.

2) Friction also acts at the <u>brakes</u> where they <u>rub</u> on the <u>rim</u> of the <u>wheel</u> or on the <u>brake disc</u>. Friction also lets you <u>grip</u> the <u>bike</u> — important if you want to ride it without slipping off.

The *Bad Points* of Friction — It *Slows* You Down

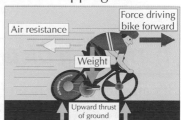

1) <u>Friction</u> always <u>wastes energy</u> — friction between the moving parts of a bike <u>warms up</u> the gears and bearings — a <u>waste</u> of energy.

2) Friction <u>limits top speed</u>. The <u>air resistance</u> (a kind of friction, see below) takes <u>most</u> of your energy and <u>limits</u> your maximum <u>speed</u>.

Air and *Water Resistance* Slow Down *Moving Objects*

1) Air and water resistance (or "drag") <u>push against</u> objects which are moving through the air or water.

2) These are kinds of <u>frictional</u> force because they try to <u>slow</u> objects down.

3) If things need to go fast, then they have to be made very <u>streamlined</u> — which just means they can <u>slip</u> through the <u>air</u> or <u>water</u> without too much resistance. A good example is a sports car.

How *Air Resistance* Affects Sheep *Jumping Out of Planes*

(It happens all the time round here.)

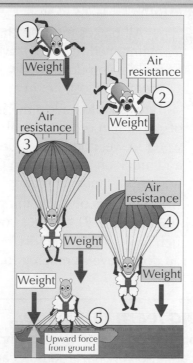

1) *Gains* Speed

At the start, the sheep only has the <u>force</u> of its <u>weight</u> (i.e. <u>gravity</u>) pulling it down — so it starts to <u>move faster</u>.

2) *Still Gaining* Speed

As it moves <u>faster</u>, the opposing force of <u>air resistance</u> gets more and more.

3) *Losing* Speed

When the parachute opens <u>air resistance increases</u> enormously — because there's a much <u>larger</u> area trying to <u>cut</u> through the air. The sheep loses speed and <u>slows down</u> gratefully.

4) *Steady* Speed

Very quickly the <u>air resistance</u> becomes <u>equal</u> to the <u>weight</u> — the two forces are <u>balanced</u>. The overall force is zero, so the sheep now moves at a <u>steady speed</u>.

5) *No* Speed

Once safely on the ground, the sheep's <u>weight</u> acting downwards is balanced by an equal <u>upward force</u> from the ground.

Stopping Distances

And now a page on stopping distances — it's a real world application of the physics of forces.

Many Factors Affect Your Total Stopping Distance

1) If you need to stop in a given distance, then the faster your vehicle's going, the bigger braking force it'll need.

2) Likewise, for any given braking force, the faster you're going, the greater your stopping distance.

3) The total stopping distance of a vehicle is the distance covered in the time between the driver first spotting a hazard and the vehicle coming to a complete stop.

4) The stopping distance is the sum of the thinking distance and the braking distance.

The reaction time is the time between the driver spotting a hazard and taking action.

1) Thinking Distance

"The distance the vehicle travels during the driver's reaction time".

It's affected by two main factors:

a) How **fast** you're going — Obviously. Whatever your reaction time, the faster you're going, the further you'll go.

b) How **aware** you are — This is affected by tiredness, drugs, alcohol and a careless attitude.

Bad visibility and distractions can also be a major factor in accidents — they might mean that a driver doesn't notice a hazard until they're quite close to it. It doesn't affect your thinking distance, but you start thinking about stopping nearer to the hazard, and so you're more likely to crash.

2) Braking Distance

"The distance the car travels under the braking force".

It's affected by four main factors:

a) How **fast** you're going — The faster you're going, the further it takes to stop.

b) How good your **brakes** are — All brakes must be checked and maintained regularly. Worn of faulty brakes will let you down badly just when you need them the most, i.e. in an emergency.

c) How good the **tyres** are — Tyres should have a minimum tread depth of 1.6 mm in order to be able to get rid of the water in wet conditions. Leaves, diesel spills and muck on the road can greatly increase the braking distance, and cause the car to skid too.

d) How good the **grip** is — This depends on three things:
1) road surface, 2) weather conditions, 3) tyres.

Wet or icy roads are always much more slippy than dry roads, but often you only discover this when you try to brake hard. You don't have as much grip, so you travel further before stopping.

The figures below for typical stopping distances are from the Highway Code. It's frightening to see just how far it takes to stop when you're going at 70 mph.

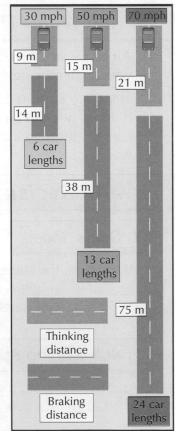

30 mph · 50 mph · 70 mph

9 m
15 m
21 m
14 m
6 car lengths
38 m
13 car lengths
75 m
Thinking distance
Braking distance
24 car lengths

Stop right there — and learn this page...

Without tread, a tyre will simply ride on a layer of water and skid very easily. This is called "aquaplaning". Snow and ice are also very hazardous because it is difficult for the tyres to get a grip.

Forces and Rotation

By rotating a lever, we can multiply the force that we're able to exert. Pretty clever stuff.

Forces Cause *Objects* to *Turn* Around *Pivots*

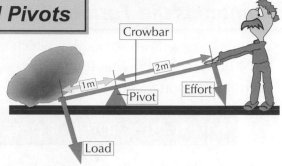

1) A <u>pivot</u> is the point around which the rotation happens — like the middle of a seesaw. A pivot is also known as a <u>fulcrum</u>.

2) A <u>lever</u> is a simple <u>machine</u>. It's called a machine because it helps us do work more <u>easily</u>. Levers often make a job of work <u>much</u> easier, by <u>multiplying</u> the <u>force</u> you put in.

3) Lifting a big rock is <u>pretty hard work</u> — but using a <u>long rod</u> as a <u>lever</u>, as shown in the diagram, makes the <u>effort force</u> required from <u>you</u> very <u>much less</u>. This is because the long lever <u>multiplies</u> the force that <u>you</u> exert.

Learn this <u>very important rule</u> about levers:

> The <u>longer</u> the <u>lever</u>, the <u>greater</u> the <u>turning force</u> about the pivot.

In other words:
the <u>longer the lever</u> on the job,
— the <u>easier the job</u> will be.
For example, take a look at these two chaps trying to undo wheel nuts.

Everyday Examples of *Levers*

Make sure you learn where to put the <u>load</u> and <u>effort</u> force arrows on these drawings. Practise sketching each drawing out until you can get it totally right.

Wheelbarrows:

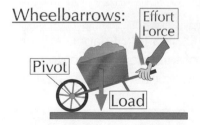

Getting lids off:

Scissors (and pliers):

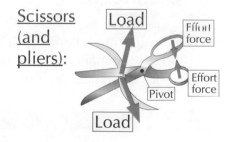

Arms:

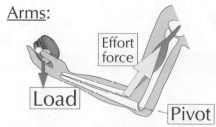

The arm acts as a lever, but it's kind of the wrong way round — the <u>effort</u> from the muscle has to be much greater than the <u>load</u>.

Doors:

Learn this stuff and may the Rotation be with you...

Make sure you understand the position of the load and effort arrows in the diagrams and you're sorted.

Moments

Don't wait a lifetime to learn moments like this — memorise what's on this page now.

A *Moment* is the *Turning Effect* of a *Force*

1) When a <u>force acts</u> on something which has a <u>pivot</u>, it creates a <u>moment</u>.

2) Learn this important equation:

$$\text{Moment} = \text{force} \times \text{perpendicular distance} \longrightarrow M = F \times d$$

in newton metres, Nm   in newtons, N   in metres, m

Balancing *Moments*

Balanced moments mean that...

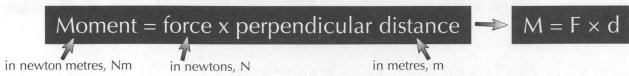

If the moments are <u>not</u> balanced, the ruler will turn in the direction of the bigger moment.

anticlockwise moments = clockwise moments

Clockwise

<u>ANTICLOCKWISE</u> force x perpendicular distance = force x perpendicular distance <u>CLOCKWISE</u>

100 N x 0.5 m = 100 N x 0.5 m

<u>50 Nm</u> = <u>50 Nm</u>   – balanced

Is it *Balanced*?

Which rulers are balanced? If you think the ruler is <u>balanced</u> write it on a bit of paper. If you reckon it's unbalanced, then write <u>unbalanced</u>, but say <u>which side</u> of the ruler will dip down. Words to use: balanced, unbalanced, left side down or right side down. Answers on page 116.

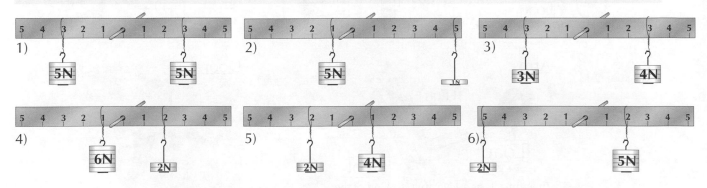

Learn all this page — it'll only take a few moments...

Nope — I don't know why they're called "moments" either. It's a good word for a short period of time, but that's about it. After that it just seems to cause confusion. It wouldn't be proper science if it all made perfect sense first time round, though. And it's a better name than rotating forcey thingy.

Pressure

Don't let pressure get you down — here's a lovely page that explains it all. That's a load off your mind.

Pressure is How Much Force is Put on a Certain Area

Pressure, force and area are all kind of tied up with each other — as the formula shows. The formula can also be put in a triangle, which is nice.

A given force acting over a big area means a small pressure (and vice versa).

$$\text{Pressure} = \frac{\text{Force}}{\text{Area}}$$

Pressure is Measured in N/m² or Pascals (Pa)

If a force of 1 newton is spread over an area of 1 m² (like this) then it exerts a pressure of 1 pascal. Simple as that.

> 1 newton/metre² = 1 pascal
> 1 N/m² = 1 Pa

Force acts normal (at 90°) to area.

Changing the Area Increases or Decreases Pressure

1) Sometimes it's helpful to decrease the pressure of something by increasing its area.

2) E.g., when people walk on snow, their feet sink down into it because the pressure is too high.

3) That's where skis come in — they increase the area of the foot, so they decrease the pressure on the snow. This makes moving in the snow much easier — they slide over the top of it.

4) Here's an example...

Downwards force of man = 600 N

Area is measured in cm² or m².

pressure = force ÷ area
= 600 N ÷ 0.1 m²
= 6000 N/m²

Area = 0.1 m²

pressure = force ÷ area
= 600 N ÷ 0.4 m²
= 1500 N/m²

Area = 0.4 m²

5) Sometimes it's helpful to increase the pressure of something by decreasing the area.

6) For example, blades need to exert large pressures to cut through materials. To do this, they have edges with a small area (sharp edges).

EXAMPLE: An axe needs to exert a pressure of 350,000,000 N/m² to chop through a log. Jack can swing the axe with a force of 3500 N. How small does the area of the blade have to be to chop through the log?

Here, you need to rearrange the pressure formula using the formula triangle at the top of the page.

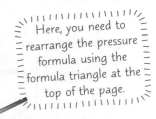

ANSWER: Area = force ÷ pressure
= 3500 N ÷ 350,000,000 N/m² = 0.00001 m²

Pressure — pushing down on you, pressing down on me...

First things first, get that formula learnt. Remember, when there is a set force, increasing the area will decrease pressure and decreasing area will increase pressure. Nothing too tricky here.

Density

You should be a whizz at formula triangles by now. Show this page who's boss.

Density is Mass per Unit Volume

1) <u>Density</u> is a measure of the '<u>compactness</u>' of a substance. It relates the <u>mass</u> of a substance to how much <u>space</u> it <u>takes up</u>.

2) The units of density are g/cm³ or kg/m³
   N.B. 1 g/cm³ = 1000 kg/m³

3) <u>Solids</u>, <u>liquids</u> and <u>gases</u> (like <u>air</u>) are made up of <u>particles</u> (page 40) so they all have mass and volume.

4) You can find the <u>density</u> of any object or substance as long as you know its <u>mass</u> and <u>volume</u>...

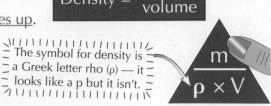

$$\text{Density} = \frac{\text{mass}}{\text{volume}}$$

The symbol for density is a Greek letter rho (ρ) — it looks like a p but it isn't.

$$\frac{m}{\rho \times V}$$

Measuring the Density of Regularly-Shaped Objects

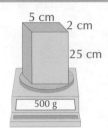

5 cm 2 cm

25 cm

500 g

Find the <u>mass</u> and <u>volume</u> and use the <u>formula</u> above like this...

Volume of a cuboid = length × width × height

Mass of object (from mass balance) = <u>500 g</u>

Volume of object = 25 cm x 5 cm x 2 cm = <u>250 cm³</u>

Density = mass ÷ volume = 500 g ÷ 250 cm³ = <u>2 g/cm³</u>

Volume is measured in cm³ or m³.

Measuring the Density of Irregularly-Shaped Objects

1) First find the <u>mass</u> of the object using a mass balance. Then it gets a bit more <u>tricky</u>...

2) Find the volume by dropping the object into a <u>measuring beaker</u> of water. The <u>change in volume</u> of the <u>water</u> is the same as the <u>volume of the object</u>.

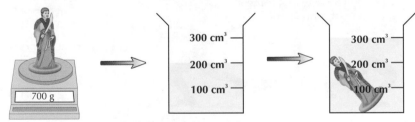

700 g

300 cm³
200 cm³
100 cm³

300 cm³
200 cm³
100 cm³

Change in water volume
= volume after – volume before
= 300 cm³ – 200 cm³
= 100 cm³

3) Now use the <u>formula</u>: Density = mass ÷ volume = 700 g ÷ 100 cm³ = <u>7 g/cm³</u>

Measuring the Density of Liquids

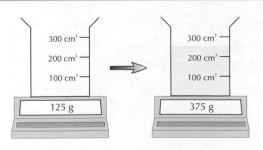

300 cm³
200 cm³
100 cm³

125 g

300 cm³
200 cm³
100 cm³

375 g

1) Find the mass of a liquid by measuring the mass of an <u>empty beaker</u>, then the mass of the <u>beaker and liquid</u>. The mass of the liquid is the same as this <u>change in mass</u>. From the diagram, <u>mass</u> = 375 g – 125 g = <u>250 g</u>

2) Find the volume of the liquid by reading off the scale. <u>Volume = 250 cm³</u>

3) Now use the <u>formula</u>:
   Density = mass ÷ volume = 250 g ÷ 250 cm³ = <u>1 g/cm³</u>

Density — Not a settlement of foxes (oh my sides)...

This is another 'get this formula learned page', so I'd do that if I were you. Make sure you know the different ways to calculate volume for different objects and liquid, as it's easy to get caught out here.

Summary Questions

Section 10 is all about forces and motion. It's all pretty straightforward stuff really and the questions below will test whether you've learnt the basic facts. If you're having trouble learning it all, try taking just one page on its own. Start by learning part of it, then covering it up and jotting it down again. Then learn a bit more and scribble that down. Soon enough you'll have learnt the whole section.

1) What exactly is speed? Write down the formula triangle for speed.

2)* A bird is leaving its nest. It flies 10 m in 2 seconds. Calculate the bird's speed.

3)* You can run 100 m in 15 seconds. Can you run faster than the bird in question 2 can fly?

4)* When a car is going at 40 mph, how far will it travel in 15 minutes?

5) What are the units of force? What would you use to measure force?

6) What are the five different things that forces can make objects do?

7) What do balanced forces produce? What do unbalanced forces do?

8) If the forces acting on a moving bus are balanced, what will happen to its speed?

9) What happens when a spring is compressed by a force and that force is removed?

10) Write down the formula for Hooke's Law.

11)* What is the spring constant for a spring which extends 5 cm with a 100 N force applied?

12)* The extension for one spring is 2 cm. What will the extension be for two identical springs in parallel?

13) What is friction? When does it occur?

14) Give three good points of friction. Give two bad points of friction.

15) What is air resistance? And water resistance?

16) A sheep jumps out a plane. What happens to its speed at first?

17) As the sheep moves faster, what happens to the air resistance acting on the sheep?

18) What happens to the air resistance when the sheep's parachute opens?

19) What is the stopping distance the sum of?

20) Over the course of a journey, Ed drives at speeds of 30 mph, 50 mph and 70 mph. Assuming identical road and weather conditions in each case, from what speed could Ed stop the quickest?

21) What is a pivot?

22) What is a moment? Give the formula for a moment.

23) Which lever could produce the biggest turning force, a 1 m lever or a 2 m lever?

24) What does "balanced moments" mean?

25)* A force of 100 N is applied to a see-saw, 1 m from the pivot. At what distance from the pivot should a force of 50 N be applied to balance the seesaw?

26) What is pressure? Give the formula for calculating pressure.

27)* A force of 200 N acts on an area of 2 m². Calculate the pressure.

28) What is density? Give the formula for calculating density.

29)* A stone brick has dimensions 10 cm x 10 cm x 3 cm. It has a mass of 1050 g. What is its density?

30)* An empty beaker has a mass of 100 g. The same beaker with 200 cm³ of liquid in it has a mass of 350 g. What is the density of the liquid?

Light

Light's fantastic — it's super-fast for a start. Here's a page all about light...

Light is a Wave of Energy

1) Light comes from <u>luminous sources</u> such as the <u>Sun</u>, <u>candles</u>, <u>light bulbs</u>, <u>flames</u> and <u>glow worms</u>.
2) Light is a <u>wave</u>, which always travels in a <u>straight line</u>.

Light Travels Faster Than Sound

1) Light travels <u>very fast</u> — much much <u>faster than sound</u>.
2) When a <u>starting pistol</u> is fired (some distance away), you <u>see</u> the smoke <u>first</u> — and <u>hear</u> the bang <u>afterwards</u>.
3) This is because <u>the light</u> reaches you <u>before</u> the <u>sound</u> does.

Light Travels Fastest in a Vacuum

1) A vacuum is where there is <u>nothing at all</u> — no <u>air</u>, no <u>particles</u>, <u>nothing</u>. <u>Space</u> is mostly a vacuum.
2) The <u>speed of light in a vacuum</u> is <u>always</u> 3×10^8 m/s (that's three hundred million metres per second). It's a <u>constant</u>.

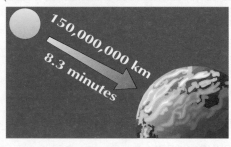

3) This means light from the Sun gets to Earth in only <u>8.3 minutes</u> — even though it's 150,000,000 km away.
4) <u>Nothing travels faster</u> than light in a vacuum.
5) Although light is <u>slower</u> when it has to travel through <u>matter</u> (like <u>air</u> or <u>water</u>), it's still <u>so fast</u> that its movement appears <u>instant</u> to the human eye.

White Light is Not Just a Single Colour

1) Bit of a shocker, I know — but white light is actually a <u>mixture</u> of <u>colours</u>.
2) This shows up when white light hits a <u>prism</u> or a <u>raindrop</u>. It gets <u>dispersed</u> (i.e. <u>split up</u>) into a full rainbow of colours.
3) The proper <u>name</u> for this <u>rainbow</u> effect is a <u>spectrum</u>.
4) Learn the <u>order</u> that the colours come out in:
   <u>Red</u> <u>Orange</u> <u>Yellow</u> <u>Green</u> <u>Blue</u> <u>Indigo</u> <u>Violet</u>
   Remember it with this <u>historical jollyism</u>:
   Richard Of York Gave Battle In Velvet

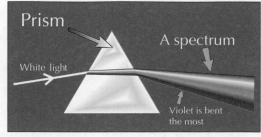

Prism

A spectrum

White light

Violet is bent the most

Confused? Let me shed some light on the problem...

So there you go. You should know now that light travels pretty flippin' fast. And you should also know why in a thunderstorm you see the lightning before you hear the thunder. And when the storm's over, you should know why you might see a beautiful rainbow. Ah, what a worthwhile page.

Reflection

Take a moment and reflect on what you're about to learn...

*We **See** Things Because **Light Reflects** Into Our **Eyes***

1) A light wave is also known as a light <u>ray</u>.

2) When <u>luminous objects</u> produce light (see previous page), it is <u>reflected back (scattered)</u> off <u>non-luminous</u> objects, e.g. you, me, books, sheep, etc.

3) Some of the reflected light then goes <u>into our eyes</u> and that, my friend, is how we see.

Mirrors** Have **Shiny Surfaces** Which **Reflect Light

1) A <u>mirror</u> has a very <u>smooth shiny surface</u>, which reflects light.

2) A <u>plane (flat) mirror</u> reflects all the light off at the <u>same angle</u>, giving a <u>clear reflection</u>.

3) Learn the <u>law of reflection</u>:

> Angle of incidence = Angle of reflection
> Angle i = Angle r

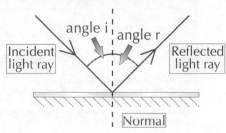

4) The <u>angle of incidence</u> and the <u>angle of reflection</u> are always measured between the <u>light ray</u> and the <u>normal</u>.

5) The <u>normal</u> is a line at a <u>right angle</u> (90°) to the surface.

This is a <u>ray diagram</u>. Make sure you draw <u>straight lines</u> and get the <u>angles</u> <u>the same</u> when drawing ray diagrams (use a <u>ruler</u> and a <u>protractor</u>).

Mirrors Are Really Useful

The fact that mirrors give a <u>clear reflection</u> is really useful. For example:

1) <u>Rear-view mirrors</u> are used in cars so that the driver can see what's going on <u>behind the car</u>.

2) <u>Periscopes</u> use mirrors to let you see <u>around an obstacle</u>. They're used in submarines, etc.

A simple periscopes is made up of <u>two mirrors</u> held in a tube — each mirror is <u>angled</u> at <u>45°</u> so that light reflects into the user's eyes.

Mirror mirror on the wall, you reflect light rays, that is all...

So light reflects off surfaces and lets us see things. Make sure there's plenty of light reflecting off this page then get learning the facts. Be sure to learn the 'Law of Reflection' and check you know how to measure angles of incidence and reflection. After that, why don't you make yourself a periscope...

Refraction

Refraction is all about light bending — nothing to do with redoing your maths homework.

Refraction is When Light Bends as it Crosses a Boundary

1) Light will travel through <u>transparent</u> (see-through) materials, but it <u>won't</u> go through anything <u>opaque</u> (not see-through).

2) Any <u>substance</u> that <u>light</u> (or another wave, e.g. sound) <u>travels through</u> is called a <u>medium</u>.

3) When light travels <u>from one</u> transparent medium <u>to another</u>, it <u>bends</u> or <u>refracts</u>.

<u>Learn these</u>:

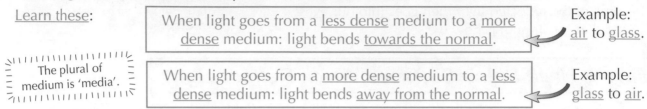

When light goes from a <u>less dense</u> medium to a <u>more dense</u> medium: light bends <u>towards the normal</u>.

Example:
<u>air</u> to <u>glass</u>.

The plural of medium is 'media'.

When light goes from a <u>more dense</u> medium to a <u>less dense</u> medium: light bends <u>away from the normal</u>.

Example:
<u>glass</u> to <u>air</u>.

Light Hitting a Glass Block is Like a Car Hitting Sand

1) <u>Light</u> hits the <u>glass</u> at an <u>angle</u>, <u>slows down</u> and <u>bends</u>.

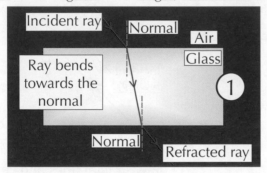

Incident ray | Normal | Air | Glass
Ray bends towards the normal
①
Normal | Refracted ray

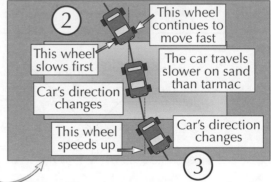

② This wheel continues to move fast
This wheel slows first
The car travels slower on sand than tarmac
Car's direction changes
This wheel speeds up
Car's direction changes
③

2) It's a bit like a <u>car</u> hitting <u>sand</u> at an angle. The right wheel get <u>slowed down first</u> and this turns the car to the <u>right</u> — <u>towards the normal</u>.

3) Leaving the sand, the right wheel <u>speeds up first</u> and this turns the car to the <u>left</u> — <u>away from the normal</u>.

4) If <u>both</u> wheels hit the sand <u>together</u> they <u>slow down together</u>, so the car goes straight through, <u>without turning</u>.

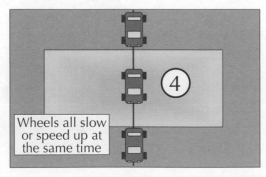

④
Wheels all slow or speed up at the same time

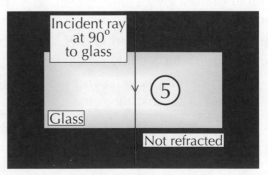

Incident ray at 90° to glass
⑤
Glass
Not refracted

5) <u>Light</u> does exactly the <u>same</u> when it hits the glass block <u>straight on</u>.

My friend thought she was a medium — but I saw through her...

Right, make sure you get your head around the stuff at the top of the page about light bending towards or away from the normal. Then check you properly understand the glass block and car examples.

Sound

Listen up — it's time to get noisy with a whole page about sound...

Light Can Travel Through a *Vacuum* but *Sound Can't*

Something Must *Vibrate* for *Sound* to *Travel*

1) Sound needs a <u>medium</u> to travel through because something has to <u>pass on</u> the sound <u>vibrations</u>.
2) Sound can travel through <u>solids</u>, <u>liquids</u> and <u>air</u>.
3) It can be <u>reflected</u> and <u>refracted</u> just like light.
4) An <u>echo</u> is sound being <u>reflected</u> from a surface.

The *Bell Jar Demo* — *Suck the Air Out* and it *Goes Quiet*

If you pop a <u>ringing alarm clock</u> in a <u>sealed jar</u>, then gradually suck out all the <u>air</u>, this is what happens:

When there <u>is</u> air in the jar:

The ringing <u>can be heard</u> through the jar because the <u>vibrating bells</u> make the air inside <u>vibrate</u>. This makes the <u>jar vibrate</u>, which in turn makes the <u>air outside vibrate</u> — and then <u>we hear it</u>.

Can hear alarm clock

When there's <u>no</u> air in the jar:

Now the alarm <u>can't be heard</u> because even though the bells are <u>clanging</u>, there's <u>no</u> air in the jar to carry the vibrations. If there's nothing there to vibrate, then <u>sound can't travel</u>.

Can't hear alarm clock in vacuum

To vacuum pump

Amplitude is the *Loudness* of *Sound*

1) If sound is 'seen' on an <u>oscilloscope</u> it looks like this — a <u>wave</u>.
2) The <u>amplitude</u> of sound is the <u>height of the wave</u>.
3) The <u>amplitude</u> shows how much <u>energy</u> the sound has.
4) A <u>large amplitude</u> means the wave has lots of energy.
5) A <u>large amplitude</u> also means the sound is <u>louder</u>. So a wave with <u>more energy</u> has a <u>bigger amplitude</u> and is <u>louder</u>.
6) A whisper has a <u>low amplitude</u> — a shout has a <u>large amplitude</u>.

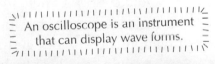

An oscilloscope is an instrument that can display wave forms.

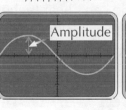

Amplitude

Bigger Amplitude

Louder

Frequency is the *Pitch* of *Sound*

1) The frequency of sound is the <u>number of complete waves</u> that pass a point per second — it's a measure of how <u>high pitched</u> the note is.
2) A <u>high frequency</u> means a <u>high pitched</u> note.
3) A <u>high frequency</u> also means more waves per second. <u>More waves per second</u> means the sound gets <u>higher pitched</u>.
4) A mooing cow produces <u>low frequency</u> sounds whilst screeching teenagers produce <u>high frequency</u> sounds. (All too frequently...)

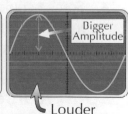

Frequency = number of these per second

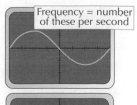

Higher pitched

The sound of silence — that's my favourite sound...

Quite a bit to learn here. Cover the page and write down the five headings to start with. Once you've got that sussed, try to get all the numbered points down too. And don't forget those wavey diagrams.

Hearing

They say gags about mishearing don't work in books. I think that's silly — I'm not fearing anything.

Sound Waves Make Your Ear Drum Vibrate

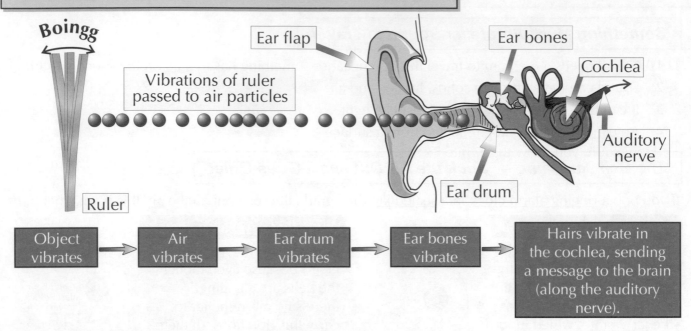

| Object vibrates | → | Air vibrates | → | Ear drum vibrates | → | Ear bones vibrate | → | Hairs vibrate in the cochlea, sending a message to the brain (along the auditory nerve). |

People Have Different Audible Ranges

1) Your <u>audible range</u> is the <u>range of frequencies</u> (vibrations per second) that you can hear.

2) The audible range of humans <u>varies a lot</u> — but it's typically <u>20-20 000 hertz (Hz)</u>.

3) This means we <u>can't hear low-pitched</u> sounds with frequencies of <u>less</u> than 20 Hz or <u>high-pitched</u> sounds <u>above</u> 20 000 Hz.

4) Some people can't hear <u>higher pitched</u> sounds. <u>Poor hearing</u> like that is caused by:

   a) <u>Wax</u> blocking ears.   c) <u>Damage</u> caused by <u>illnesses</u> and <u>infections</u>.
   b) <u>Nerve</u> damage.   d) <u>Old age</u> and general <u>deterioration</u>.

Loud Noises Can Damage Hearing

1) Loudness is measured in <u>decibels</u> (dB).

2) <u>Hearing</u> can be <u>damaged</u> by noises <u>above 85 dB</u>.

3) A sudden <u>really loud noise</u> (like an <u>explosion</u>) can <u>burst the ear drum</u> or <u>damage ear bones</u>.

4) Being around loud noise over a <u>long period of time</u> (such as noisy <u>machinery</u> or <u>loud music</u>) can damage the <u>hairs</u> in the ear.

5) Damage to your hearing may mean that you struggle to hear things properly because they sound <u>muffled</u> or <u>too quiet</u>.

6) Damage can be <u>temporary</u> or <u>permanent</u>.

20 dB   40 dB   60 dB   110 dB   120 dB
Ear Damage Likely

Save 50% on your audible range — chop an ear off...

That diagram at the top of the page is a bit of a blockbuster isn't it? I reckon you should learn what all the labels are. All the stuff about hearing damage is pretty interesting too. I'd say it's definitely a bad idea to have music blasting out of your earphones — you could be gradually damaging your hearing.

Summary Questions

Well, that was Section 11, a humdinger of a section all about light and sound. There are quite a few words in there — and some pretty important diagrams too. That's a lot of facts to learn, I know, and you're bound to find some of them tricky to remember. But, (as somebody famous once said) "Nothing in the world can take the place of persistence" — in other words, if you want to achieve anything difficult, there's no other option than keep on slogging away at it...

1) What term is used to describe things that produce light?

2) Which travels fastest, light or sound? Give a piece of evidence which shows this.

3) Where does light travel fastest?

4) How could you show that white light is not just one colour?

5) Write down a sentence that you could use to help you remember the order of the colours in a spectrum.

6) Describe how light gets from the Sun to an object and then to our eyes.

7) What is a mirror?

8) What is the 'Law of Reflection'?

9) Sketch a diagram of a periscope.

10) What is refraction?

11) If you were talking about light and sound waves, what would you mean by 'a medium'?

12) What happens when light goes from a less dense medium to a more dense medium?

13) What happens when light goes from a more dense medium to a less dense medium?

14) What is an echo?

15) Why can't you hear a ringing bell in a vacuum?

16) If you were to 'see' a sound wave on an oscilloscope, which bit would show the amplitude?

17) What does the amplitude of a wave tell you?

18) Which would have a larger amplitude — a shout or a whisper?

19) What does the frequency of a sound mean?

20) Which would have a higher frequency — a high pitched note or a low pitched note?

21) Draw a labelled diagram of an ear.

22) Explain how you would hear a ruler being flicked on a table edge.

23) What does audible range mean?

24) What is the typical audible range of humans?

25) What is loudness measured in? At what level of loudness might ear damage start?

26) Describe how a sudden loud noise might damage the ear.

27) Describe how being around loud noise over a long period of time might damage the ear.

Section 11 — Light and Sound

Gravity and the Sun

It's not magic that keeps your feet on the ground, it's gravity. As Sandra Bullock will tell you.

Gravity *is a* **Force** *that* **Attracts** *All* **Masses**

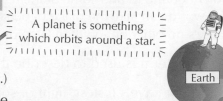

A planet is something which orbits around a star.

Earth

1) Anything with <u>mass</u> will <u>attract</u> anything else with mass. In other words, everything in the Universe is attracted by the force of <u>gravity</u> to everything else. (But you only notice it when one of the things is really big like a planet.)

2) You're <u>attracted to the Earth</u> by gravity. There's a constant force, pulling you towards the <u>centre of the Earth</u> at all times.

3) The <u>more massive</u> the object (or body) — the <u>stronger</u> the force of gravity is (so planets with a <u>large mass</u> have <u>high gravity</u>).

← weak attraction →

Earth   Neptune

4) The <u>further the distance</u> between objects — the <u>weaker</u> the gravitational attraction becomes.

Gravity *Keeps the* **Solar System** *Together*

There's more about our Solar System on the next page.

1) The <u>Sun</u> (at the <u>centre</u> of our <u>Solar System</u>) is a <u>star</u>. The <u>Earth</u> is one of <u>eight</u> planets which orbit the Sun.

2) The Sun is really <u>huge</u> and has a big <u>mass</u> — so its <u>gravity</u> is really <u>strong</u>.

3) The pull from the Sun's gravity is what keeps all the planets in their <u>orbits</u>. The planets all move in <u>elliptical orbits</u> (elongated circles) around the Sun.

4) The pull from <u>Earth's gravity</u> is what keeps the <u>Moon</u> in its orbit.

Gravity *Gives You* **Weight** *— But* **Not Mass**

To understand this you must <u>learn all these facts</u> about <u>mass and weight</u>:

1) <u>Mass</u> is just the <u>amount of 'stuff'</u> in an object. The mass of an object <u>never changes</u>, no matter where it is in the Universe.

2) <u>Weight</u> is caused by the <u>pull</u> of <u>gravity</u>.

3) An object has the <u>same mass</u> whether it's on <u>Earth</u> or on <u>another planet</u> (or on a <u>star</u>) — but its <u>weight</u> will be <u>different</u>. For example, a 1 kg mass will <u>weigh less</u> on <u>Mars</u> than it does on <u>Earth</u>, simply because the <u>force</u> of gravity pulling on it is <u>less</u>.

Weight is a <u>force</u> measured in <u>newtons</u> (N). It's measured using a <u>spring</u> balance or <u>newton meter</u>. <u>Mass</u> is <u>not</u> a force. It's measured in <u>kilograms</u> (kg) with a <u>mass</u> balance.

Stars *Give Out* **Light**, *Planets* **Don't**

Note: Mass balances, like this, only work on Earth.

1) The <u>Sun</u> and other <u>stars</u> are <u>light sources</u> — they give out light.

2) The Sun gives out a <u>massive</u> amount of <u>light</u> (and heat).

3) The <u>planets</u> and the <u>Moon</u> are <u>not</u> light sources — we can only see them because they <u>reflect</u> the Sun's light.

Just make sure you appreciate the gravity of all this...

Remember: weight and mass are not the same — weight is caused by the pull of gravity on a mass.

The Solar System and Beyond

Ahh. This is going to be a nice page, I can tell. Look at all those lovely big pictures for a start.

The **Sun** is at the **Centre** of Our **Solar System**

You need to know the <u>order</u> of the planets from the Sun — do it by learning this little jollyism:

Mercury	Venus	Earth	Mars	Jupiter	Saturn	Uranus	Neptune
My	Very	Early	Morning	Journey	Started	Up	North

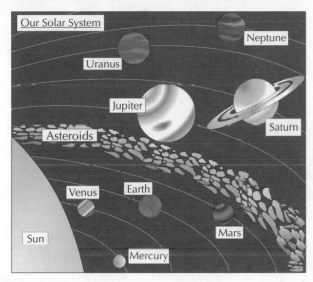

This table gives you an idea of <u>how far</u> each planet is from the Sun.

	Planet	Mean Distance From Sun (millions of km)
INNER PLANETS	Mercury	58
	Venus	108
	Earth	150
	Mars	228
OUTER PLANETS	Jupiter	778
	Saturn	1430
	Uranus	2870
	Neptune	4500

Beyond the **Solar System**

1) A <u>galaxy</u> is a <u>large collection</u> of <u>stars</u>. The <u>Universe</u> is made up of <u>billions</u> of galaxies.

2) Our <u>Solar System</u> and most of the stars you see at night are in a <u>galaxy</u> called the <u>Milky Way</u>. The other galaxies are all <u>so far away</u> they just look like <u>small fuzzy stars</u>.

A **Light Year** is How Far **Light** Travels in **One Year**

1) Space is really, <u>really</u> big. Objects in space are <u>so far away</u> from each other that scientists use a special unit called the <u>light year</u> to measure distances in space.

2) A light year is how far <u>light travels in one year</u> (and remember <u>nothing</u> travels faster than light — see page 90).

3) For example, even though <u>Proxima Centauri</u> is our second-closest star (the closest is the Sun of course), it is still <u>4 light years</u> away. That means it takes light <u>4 years</u> to travel from the star to <u>Earth</u> — it's a looooooooooong way.

Proxima Centauri

4 light years

Earth

1 light year ≈ 9.5 million million km (a <u>long</u> way)

Galaxies, the Milky Way — physicists must like chocolate...

See, I told you this would be a nice page. So there's absolutely no excuse for not learning everything on it. You know the score by now. Cover up the page and scribble down everything you can remember. Then check back over the page to see what you missed. Then try again, till you get it all.

The Movement of the Earth

In years to come, this stuff will come up in a quiz and you'll be able to wow your teammates with the answer. You also need to know it for your exam. So get cracking...

Day and Night are Due to the Steady Rotation of the Earth

1) The Earth does <u>one complete rotation</u> in <u>24 hours</u>. That's what a <u>day</u> actually is — <u>one complete rotation of the Earth</u> about its axis.

2) The Sun doesn't really move, so as the Earth rotates, any place on its surface (like the UK, say) will <u>sometimes face the Sun</u> (<u>day time</u>) and other times <u>face away</u> into dark space (<u>night time</u>).

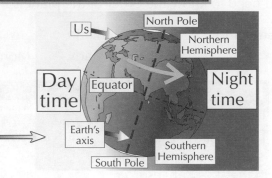

The Seasons are Caused by the Earth's Tilt

1) The Earth takes <u>365 ¼ days</u> to <u>orbit once</u> around the Sun. That's one year of course. (The extra ¼ day is sorted out every <u>leap year</u>.)

2) Each year has <u>four seasons</u>. The seasons are caused by the <u>tilt</u> of the <u>Earth's axis</u>.

A leap year has an extra day added. We have one every 4 years.

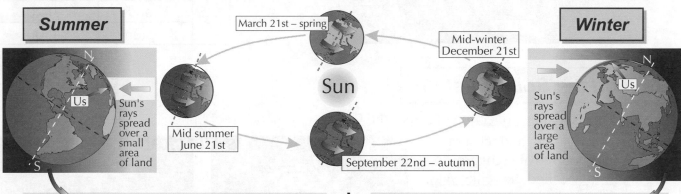

Summer

Sun's rays spread over a small area of land

Mid summer June 21st

March 21st – spring

Sun

September 22nd – autumn

Mid-winter December 21st

Winter

Sun's rays spread over a large area of land

1) When it's summer in the UK, the <u>northern hemisphere</u> (everything above the equator) is tilted <u>towards</u> the Sun.

2) The northern half of the Earth spends <u>more time in sunlight</u> than it does in darkness, i.e. <u>days are longer</u> than nights. Longer days mean <u>more hours of sunshine</u> — so the land <u>heats up</u>.

3) Not only that, but the Sun's rays cover a <u>small area</u> of land. This means that the <u>heat</u> is <u>focused</u> on a small area. So it gets <u>warm</u> and we have summer — hoorah.

1) When it's winter in the UK, the northern hemisphere is tilted <u>away</u> from the Sun.

2) The north now spends <u>less time in sunlight</u> so <u>days are shorter</u> than nights.

3) Also, the Sun's rays cover a <u>larger area</u> of land so the heat is <u>more spread out</u>. So it gets <u>colder</u> and we have <u>winter</u>.

When it's <u>summer</u> in the <u>northern hemisphere</u>, it's <u>winter</u> in the <u>southern hemisphere</u> — and vice versa.

Phew — I feel quite giddy now...

Well this is all very jolly. Not like usual boring old science at all. This is really interesting. OK. Fairly interesting. Anyway, learn the headings, the diagrams, the details — and scribble. Make sure you know how the tilt of the Earth's axis gives us warm summers (yeah, right) and cold winters.

The Movement of the Earth

People used to think that the Earth stayed still and everything else moved around it. Now we know that the Earth moves through space and rotates, which makes it look like everything else is moving around it.

The **Sun** Doesn't Move — the **Earth Rotates**

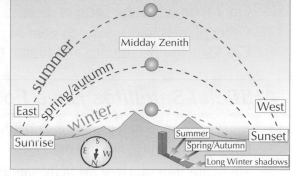

1) The Sun "rises" in the <u>EAST</u> and "sets" in the <u>WEST</u>. It seems like this to us because the <u>Earth is rotating</u>.

2) The Sun is <u>highest</u> in the sky at <u>midday</u>. (12.00 noon in winter, but 1.00 pm in British Summer Time.)

3) So <u>shadows</u> are always <u>shortest</u> at <u>midday</u>. This is because the Earth is <u>tilted</u> on its axis.

4) The <u>tilt</u> of the Earth affects the <u>seasons</u> (see previous page) and the <u>height</u> of the Sun in the sky changes from season to season.

5) The sun is <u>highest</u> in the sky during <u>summer</u> and <u>lowest</u> during <u>winter</u>.

6) So shadows are <u>shorter</u> in <u>summer</u> than winter.

The **Stars** Look Like They Move Too — **But They Don't**

1) The picture on the right is like a <u>long exposure</u> taken over <u>several hours</u> at night. It shows that the stars <u>seem to move</u> in <u>circular paths</u> around the night sky.

2) This is all simply caused by the <u>rotation of the Earth</u>.

3) The <u>Pole Star</u> in the north of the sky stays "<u>fixed</u>" and the other stars "rotate" slowly around it. This is because the Pole Star is <u>directly above</u> the Earth's <u>axis of rotation</u>. This makes it really handy for navigation.

Eclipses Happen When **Light** From the **Sun** is **Blocked**

Solar Eclipse — an Eclipse of the Sun

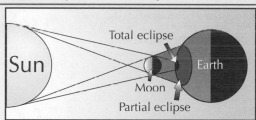

Total eclipse
Sun
Earth
Moon
Partial eclipse

1) A <u>solar eclipse</u> is when the <u>Moon passes</u> between the Sun and the Earth, <u>blocking</u> the Sun's light from reaching Earth.

2) Some places will see a <u>total eclipse</u> (when all of the Sun's light is blocked) and some will see a <u>partial eclipse</u> (when only some of the light is blocked).

Lunar Eclipse — an Eclipse of the Moon

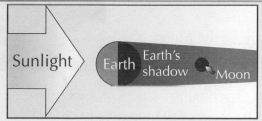

Sunlight
Earth Earth's shadow Moon

1) A <u>lunar eclipse</u> is when the <u>Earth passes</u> between the Sun and the Moon, <u>blocking</u> the Sun's light from reaching the Moon.

2) This means it looks like the <u>Moon disappears</u>.

3) Lunar eclipses can be <u>total or partial</u>.

Aaaargh — the Sun's been eaten by a giant sky monster...

If you ever get the chance to see a total solar eclipse, it's amazing (but don't look directly at the Sun). If you want to see it in the UK though, don't buy your popcorn yet — you'll have to wait 'til 2090...

Satellites

Everyone's heard of satellite TV but did you know the Moon is also a satellite?

A **Satellite** *is Something Which* **Orbits Round a Planet**

1) Moons are "natural satellites" — because they're natural objects which orbit around planets.
2) Our Moon orbits the Earth in 28 days.
3) Other planets in our Solar System have moons.
   E.g. Mars has two moons and Jupiter has 63 (talk about being greedy).

Artificial Satellites *Have* **Four Main Uses**

1) An artificial satellite is an object that people have put into orbit around the Earth.
2) There are thousands of artificial satellites orbiting above our heads. These are the four main things that they're used for:

> **1** Communication and Navigation — Radio, TV and telephone signals are relayed around the world. Satellites are also used for GPS (Global Positioning System) — what satnavs use to pinpoint their location.

> **3** Observing the Earth — Spy satellites have military uses and satellite imaging helps to map the land and monitor the environment.

> **2** Monitoring the Weather — Weather systems are observed to help weather forecasting.

> **4** Exploring the Solar System — E.g. the Hubble telescope orbits Earth. From there it gets a clear look at the Universe without our atmosphere getting in the way.

Probes *are* **Unmanned Spacecraft**

1) Scientists send unmanned spacecraft called probes to explore other parts of our Solar System.
2) Its a cheaper and safer way to explore space than sending astronauts — for example, you don't have to worry about oxygen or food for the astronauts.
3) So far probes have visited all the planets in our Solar System. Some have even landed on the surface of Mars, Venus and Titan (one of Saturn's moons).

A **Brief History** *of* **Human Space Flight**

Humans have been fascinated by space for years, but it's only recently that we've been able to escape Earth's gravity and send people into space.

- 1961 — Yuri Gagarin became the first human in space.
- 1969 — Neil Armstrong becomes the first human to walk on the Moon.
- 1971 — The first space station is launched. A space station is an artificial satellite that orbits around Earth. Astronauts can live on a space station for a long time and carry out research and experiments.

A space station

- The future — The next big step in human space exploration is to send humans to Mars.

Satellites — in reality, they're actually quite heavy...

This page is pretty fun really — space travel and spy satellites. You don't need to know all the names and dates in that last bit, you just need to have an idea of how space exploration has developed over the years.

Summary Questions

Section 12 only has five pages of information — not much really, considering it deals with the whole Universe. It's amazing just how many people go their whole lives and never really know the answers to all those burning questions, like what is gravity? Or why are the days longer in summer than in winter? Make sure you learn all the burning answers now...

1) What is gravity?

2) How does the mass of a planet affect its gravitational strength?

3) How are all the planets kept in orbit around the Sun?

4) What is the difference between weight and mass?

5) What is weight measured in? What is mass measured in?

6) Why can we see the planets and the Moon, even though they don't give out light?

7) What is at the centre of our Solar System?

8) Write down the names of all the planets in our Solar System, starting with the one closest to the Sun.

9) What is a galaxy?

10) What is the name of our galaxy?

11) What is a light year?

12) How long does it take for the Earth to complete one full rotation on its own axis?

13) Explain what "day time" and "night time" actually are.

14) Do all places on the Earth have "day time" at the same time?

15) How long does it take for the Earth to complete one full orbit around the Sun?

16) How many seasons are there?

17) Why are days longer than nights in summer?

18) Give two reasons why it's (supposedly) hotter in Britain in summer than winter.

19) When it's summer in the northern hemisphere, what season is it in the southern hemisphere? Explain why.

20) In which part of the sky does the Sun rise? In which part of the sky does it set?

21) At what time of the day is the Sun highest in the sky?

22) At what time of day are shadows always shortest?

23) In which season does the Sun get highest in the sky?

24) In which season are shadows generally longest?

25) Why do photos of the Pole Star show circular paths for other stars around it?

26) What is a solar eclipse? What is a lunar eclipse?

27) What is a satellite?

28) How long does it take for the Moon to orbit the Earth?

29) What are artificial satellites?

30) What four things are artificial satellites used for?

31) Give two reasons why scientists might use probes, rather than astronauts, to explore space

32) Name three important steps in the history of human space flight.

Energy Transfer

Ah, energy transfer. Everything you do involves energy transfer, which makes this page very important.

Eight Forms of *Energy*

There are <u>eight</u> forms of <u>energy</u>. Here are some <u>examples</u> of each type:

Electrical Energy

Wherever there's a <u>current</u> flowing, there's <u>electrical energy</u>.

Light Energy

Anything <u>luminous</u> gives off <u>light energy</u> — things like the Sun, light bulbs, candles and glow worms.

Sound Energy

Anything <u>noisy</u> gives off <u>sound energy</u> — things like vocal chords, speakers and musical instruments.

Chemical Energy

Anything with <u>energy</u> which can be released by a <u>chemical reaction</u> — things like food, fuels and batteries.

Gravitational Energy

Anything in a <u>gravitational field</u> (i.e. anything that can <u>fall</u>) has <u>gravitational energy</u> — the <u>higher</u> it goes, the <u>more</u> it has.

Thermal Energy

<u>Everything</u> has some <u>thermal (heat) energy</u> — the <u>hotter</u> an object is, the <u>higher</u> its <u>temperature</u> and the <u>more</u> thermal energy it has.

Kinetic Energy

Anything that <u>moves</u> has <u>kinetic energy</u>.

Elastic (Strain) Energy

When you <u>deform</u> an elastic object (apply a force to change its shape) it will build up <u>elastic energy</u>. Anything <u>stretched</u> has <u>elastic energy</u> — things like rubber bands, springs, etc.

Energy Can Be **Transferred** *Between Forms*

1) Whenever (pretty much) anything happens to an object, <u>energy</u> is <u>transferred</u> from one form to another — one type of energy <u>increases</u> and another type of energy <u>decreases</u>.

2) For example:

  - When you turn on a <u>lamp</u>, you complete an electrical circuit. The lamp then emits <u>light</u> and <u>heat</u>. So <u>electrical energy</u> is transformed into <u>light</u> and <u>thermal energy</u>.
  - A <u>wind turbine</u> transforms <u>kinetic energy</u> from the wind to <u>electrical energy</u>, and a little <u>sound energy</u> (those things are noisier than you'd think).

Energy Can Be **Stored**

1) <u>Gravitational</u>, <u>chemical</u> and <u>strain energy</u> are types of <u>stored</u> energy.

2) <u>Fuel</u>, e.g. coal, stores <u>chemical energy</u>. When you <u>burn</u> the fuel, it transfers chemical energy to <u>heat</u> and <u>light energy</u>.

Coal (stored chemical energy)

3) A <u>stretched object</u>, like a <u>spring</u>, has a lot of stored <u>elastic energy</u>. When it's released, the elastic strain energy <u>decreases</u> quickly and becomes <u>kinetic energy</u>.

Start of a new section — I'm feeling energised...

Betcha didn't know energy could be so much fun. Cover up the page and check you know the eight different forms of energy. Make sure you've sussed how energy can be transferred and stored too.

Conservation of Energy

Get ready — here comes another page that's all about energy...

The *Law* of *Conservation of Energy*

Scientists have only been studying energy for about two or three hundred years so far, and in that short space of time they've already come up with two "Pretty Important Principles" relating to energy: Learn them really well:

> THE LAW OF CONSERVATION OF ENERGY
> Energy can never be created nor destroyed
> — it's only ever transferred from one form to another.

That means energy never simply disappears — it always transfers into another form. This is another very useful principle:

> Energy is only useful when it's transferred from one form to another.

Think about it — all useful machines use one kind of energy and give out another.

Most *Energy Transfers* are Not Perfect

1) Useful devices are useful because they transfer energy from one form to another.

2) Some energy is always lost in some way, nearly always as heat. When this happens, we say energy has been dissipated (spread out and lost).

3) This means that you never get as much useful energy out as you put in.

4) As the diagram shows, the energy input will always end up coming out partly as useful energy and partly as wasted energy — but no energy is destroyed:

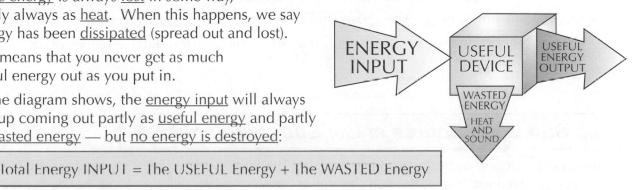

> Total Energy INPUT = The USEFUL Energy + The WASTED Energy

Two *Very Serious* Examples

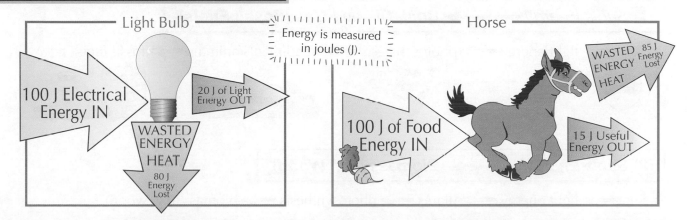

No mum I'm not slacking — I'm just conserving energy...

This stuff's super important, so make sure you can wrap your head around it before ploughing on. Remember, energy's only ever transferred to other forms. No matter how hard you try, you can't ever create or destroy energy. It's just impossible. Futile. 100% completely out of the question.

Energy Resources

The Sun's a useful little critter. It provides us with oodles of energy and asks for nothing in return.

We Burn Fuels for Energy

See page 102 for more on all the different types of energy.

1) Most of the energy we use is stored as chemical energy in fuels.

2) When we burn fuels, the energy is released as thermal energy.

3) We can transfer this energy into other forms of energy, like electrical energy (see page 102). We can also use the thermal energy directly, e.g. to heat houses.

4) Fuels include biomass (e.g. wood) and fossil fuels (e.g. coal, oil and natural gas).

5) Batteries also store energy as chemical energy. To release the energy they contain we connect them up to an electrical circuit rather than burning them (see page 73).

Fossil Fuels Come from Long-Dead Plants and Animals

1) Millions of years ago, plants on Earth were capturing the Sun's energy using photosynthesis (see page 24). There were also animals that got energy from eating plants (and other animals).

2) Some of this energy was stored up in the tissues of these plants and animals.

3) After they had died, their remains gradually got buried under layers of mud, rock and sand.

4) The remains slowly decayed and over millions of years the pressure turned them into fossil fuels.

5) These fuels contain the chemical energy that was originally stored in the tissues of the plants and animals.

The Sun is the Source of Our Energy Resources

Most energy around us originates from the Sun. The Sun's heat and light energy is useful for supplying our energy demands. Often the Sun's energy is transferred into different forms before we use it.

Learn all of the energy transfer chains below and on the next page.

1) Sun's Energy ⟶ Coal, Oil, and Gas (Fossil Fuels)

 Sun ⟹ light energy ⟹ photosynthesis ⟹ dead plants/animals ⟹ fossil fuels

2) Sun's Energy ⟶ Biomass (e.g. Wood)

 Sun ⟹ light energy ⟹ plants ⟹ photosynthesis ⟹ biomass (e.g. wood)

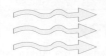 

Energy Resources

3) Sun's Energy ➜ Food

Sun ➜ light energy ➜ plants ➜ photosynthesis ➜ biomass (food)

 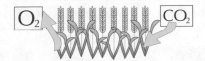

4) Sun's Energy ➜ Wind Power

Sun ➜ heats atmosphere ➜ air circulates ➜ causes winds

1) Winds are caused by <u>differences in temperature</u>.

2) The Sun <u>heats up</u> some parts of the Earth's surface more than others.

3) Above the <u>warmer</u> bits of land (or sea) you get pockets of <u>warm air</u>.

4) This warm air <u>rises</u> (because it's <u>lighter</u> than cold air).

5) When it rises, <u>cold air</u> will <u>rush in</u> to fill its place, causing a <u>wind to blow</u>.

> You can use the <u>kinetic</u> energy from wind and waves to turn turbines to generate electricity (see page 106).

5) Sun's Energy ➜ Wave Power

Sun ➜ heats atmosphere ➜ causes winds ➜ causes winds

1) The Sun causes <u>winds</u> to blow across the surface of the Earth (see above).

2) When these winds blow across the surface of the <u>sea</u>, they push the water about, creating <u>waves</u>.

The Sun Drives the Water Cycle

1) The <u>water cycle</u> also relies on <u>heat</u> from the Sun to keep going.

2) The Sun warms up water in seas, lakes and rivers, causing it to <u>evaporate</u> and turn into <u>water vapour</u>.

> 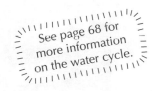 See page 68 for more information on the water cycle.

3) As the water vapour <u>rises</u> it <u>cools down</u>. Eventually it <u>condenses</u> into lots of tiny droplets of liquid water — otherwise known as <u>clouds</u>.

4) Then the water falls to the ground again as <u>rain</u>, <u>snow</u>, or <u>hail</u>, etc.

Baby you light up my world like nobody else...

...the way you give energy gets me overwhelmed. The Sun's amazing — don't take it for granted because it supplies nearly all the energy we have here on Earth. Whether it's fossil fuels, biomass, food, wind power or wave power — in the end, it's the Sun behind them all. Incredible.

Generating Electricity

We can use the energy we get from the Sun to generate electricity in lots of different ways...

We Can *Generate Electricity* by *Burning Fuels*

1) At the moment we generate most of our electricity by burning <u>fossil fuels</u> (coal, oil and gas). This diagram shows how it's done:

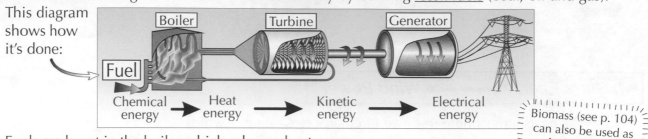

Boiler | Turbine | Generator

Fuel

Chemical energy → Heat energy → Kinetic energy → Electrical energy

Biomass (see p. 104) can also be used as a fuel to generate electricity in this way.

2) <u>Fuels</u> are <u>burnt</u> in the <u>boiler</u> which releases <u>heat energy</u>.

3) This is used to heat up <u>water</u> which then changes to <u>high pressure steam</u>.

4) The steam is then used to drive huge <u>turbines</u> which are just like really big <u>fans</u>.

5) The <u>turbines</u> are attached to a <u>generator</u>, which spins and transfers <u>kinetic energy</u> into <u>electrical energy</u>.

6) <u>Nuclear power stations</u> also use steam to turn turbines and power a generator — but they use <u>radioactivity</u> from the nuclear fuel <u>uranium</u> to produce the <u>heat energy</u>.

There Are *Other Ways* of *Generating Electricity...*

Wind Power

1) This involves putting <u>lots of windmills</u> (wind turbines) up in <u>exposed places</u> like on <u>moors</u> or round <u>coasts</u>.

2) Each wind turbine has its own <u>generator</u> inside it so the electricity is generated <u>directly</u> from the <u>wind</u> turning the <u>blades</u>, which <u>turn the generator</u>.

The wind drives the turbines directly — no need for steam.

Hydroelectric Power

1) <u>Hydroelectric power</u> usually requires <u>flooding</u> a <u>valley</u> by building a <u>big dam</u>.

2) <u>Rainwater</u> is caught and allowed out <u>through turbines</u>, driving them directly. The turbines then drive generators to make <u>electricity</u>.

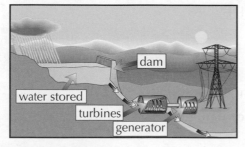

dam

water stored

turbines

generator

Wave Power

1) You need lots of small <u>wave-powered turbines</u> located <u>around the coast</u>.

2) As waves come in to the shore they create an <u>up and down motion</u> that can be used to turn a <u>turbine</u>.

3) The turbine drives a <u>generator</u>.

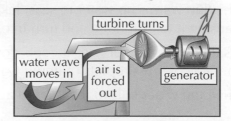

turbine turns

water wave moves in | air is forced out | generator

Solar Power

1) <u>Solar cells</u> generate <u>electric currents directly</u> from sunlight.

2) Solar cells are usually used to generate electricity on a <u>relatively small scale</u>, e.g. powering <u>individual homes</u>.

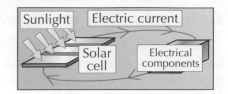

Sunlight | Electric current

Solar cell | Electrical components

Generating Electricity

Electricity can be generated with non-renewable or renewable energy resources...

Non-renewable *Energy Resources* Will Run Out

<u>Non-renewable</u> energy resources include <u>fossil fuels</u> and <u>nuclear fuel</u>. We use them up much <u>faster</u> than they're produced so eventually our supply will <u>run out</u>. They have advantages and disadvantages:

Advantages

1) Non-renewable energy resources produce a <u>lot of energy</u>.

2) They do not rely on the <u>weather</u>, unlike most renewable resources.

3) We have lots of fossil fuel power stations already, so we <u>don't</u> need to spend money on new technology to carry on using them.

Disadvantages

1) There's a <u>limited supply</u> of them.

2) Burning fossil fuels releases a lot of <u>carbon dioxide</u> into the atmosphere, which can contribute to <u>global warming</u> and <u>climate change</u> (see page 69).

3) Burning coal and oil also releases <u>sulfur dioxide</u>, which causes <u>acid rain</u> (see page 69).

4) Nuclear power stations produce <u>radioactive waste</u> — this can be very <u>dangerous</u> and difficult to <u>dispose of</u>.

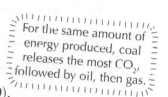
For the same amount of energy produced, coal releases the most CO_2, followed by oil, then gas.

Renewable *Energy Resources* Won't Run Out

<u>Renewable</u> energy resources are ones which won't <u>run out</u>, e.g. biomass, wind, waves, etc. Just like non-renewable energy resources, they have advantages and disadvantages:

Advantages

1) They will <u>never run out</u> — as long as the sun shines we'll always have renewable energy resources (see pages 104-105).

2) They can <u>damage the environment</u> (see below), but in <u>less nasty</u> ways than non-renewables.

3) Once the equipment has been set up, there are <u>minimal running costs</u> and the fuel is <u>free</u>.

4) They create <u>little or no pollution</u> once they're up and running.

Disadvantages

1) They <u>don't provide as much energy</u> as non-renewable resources.

2) They can be <u>unreliable</u> if they depend on the <u>weather</u> — e.g. wind turbines only work when it's windy, solar cells only work when it's sunny, etc.

3) They can change or sometimes damage the <u>local environment</u>. E.g. <u>wind turbines</u> can change a nice <u>view</u> and some <u>hydroelectric power</u> schemes need valleys to be <u>flooded</u>, which can destroy habitats for <u>wildlife</u>.

4) It <u>costs a lot at first</u> to set up the equipment needed to generate power from renewables.

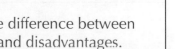

Think on pal — this'll affect all your generation...

Make sure you know the different ways that electricity can be generated and the difference between non-renewable and renewable energy resources — both have their advantages and disadvantages.

Summary Questions

Ah, the summary questions — on the home stretch at last. In this section, you got to go on a voyage of discovery into the weird and wonderful world of all things energy. All that's left for you now is to work through the exciting questions below and claim your free ice cream at the start of the next section. OK, the ice cream is a lie, but you won't regret taking the time to work through these questions if you want to be super-amazing at science, trust me. Take your time with them if you like, and maybe have the odd cheeky peek back at the appropriate page if you're stuck — I won't tell anyone, honest.

1) What are the eight main types of energy?
   Give an example of something that has each type of energy.

2) Describe the energy transformation that takes place when you switch on an electric lamp.

3) What does a wind turbine transform kinetic energy to?

4) What kind of energy is stored in a stretched spring?

5) Give two other kinds of energy that can be stored.

6) What is the Law of Conservation of Energy?

7) Why is it important that devices transfer energy from one form to another?

8) Why are most energy transfers NOT perfect?

9) What form of energy is wasted energy usually lost as?

10) How does the Sun's energy get stored in fossil fuels?

11) How does the Sun's energy give us wind power?

12) Other than fossils fuels and wind power, give two energy resources created using the Sun's energy.

13) Describe how we generate electricity from fossil fuels.

14) How do we generate electricity from wave power?

15) How do solar cells give us power?

16) Describe what is meant by 'a non-renewable energy resource'.

17) Give two examples of non-renewable energy resources.

18) Give three advantages and three disadvantages of non-renewable energy resources.

19) What are renewable energy resources?

20) Why might renewable energy resources be cheaper than non-renewable energy resources?

21) Give two other advantages of renewable energy resources.

22) Give one example of how a renewable energy resource can have a negative effect on the environment.

23) Other than the effect on the environment, give two disadvantages of using renewable energy resources.

Glossary

We've gathered up some of the most important words you need to know here, so you can remind yourself what they're all about. Words in the definitions that are underlined have their own entry.

Accurate result
A result that is very close to the true answer.

Acid rain
Acidic rain formed when pollutants such as sulfur dioxide mix with clouds.

Adaptation
A feature of an organism that makes it better suited to its environment.

Adolescence
The period of life in which a child develops into an adult.

Aerobic respiration
Respiration using oxygen. Carbon dioxide and water are produced in this reaction.

Air resistance (or drag)
Air pushing back against you when you move through it.

Alloy
A combination of different metals.

Alveoli
Small air sacs in the lungs where gas exchange takes place.

Ammeter
An instrument used to measure current — must be connected in series.

Amphibian
A vertebrate that lays eggs in water, has smooth skin and is cold-blooded (e.g. a frog).

Amplitude (of sound)
A measure of the loudness of sound.

Amylase
A digestive enzyme that is involved in breaking down starch into simple sugars.

Anhydrous
A substance that does not contain water.

Anomalous result
A result that doesn't seem to fit with the rest of the data.

Antagonistic muscles
Pairs of muscles that work against each other around a joint (e.g. the biceps and triceps).

Anther
A male part of a flower, which contains pollen grains.

Antibody
A protein produced by white blood cells. Antibodies bind to antigens on the surface of microorganisms that have entered the body and kill them.

Antigen
A molecule found on the surface of a cell. Antigens not belonging to the body trigger the production of antibodies.

Arachnid
An arthropod that has 8 legs, a 2-part body and no wings or antennae (e.g. a spider).

Arthropod
An invertebrate that has many pairs of jointed legs, a body that is divided into segments, and a hard exoskeleton (e.g. an insect).

Atom
A tiny particle that makes up all matter.

Audible range
The range of frequencies that you can hear.

Auditory nerve
A nerve in the inner ear that sends messages about sound vibrations to the brain.

Balanced diet
A diet which contains the right amount of carbohydrates, proteins, fats, vitamins, minerals, fibre and water.

Boiling
The change in state of a liquid to a gas, when it is heated to its boiling point.

Breathing
The process of getting air in and out of the lungs.

Carpel
The female part of a flower (consists of the stigma, style and ovary).

Cell surface membrane
The thin skin around a cell that holds it together and controls what goes in and out.

Cell wall
The rigid outer coating of a plant cell. It supports the cell.

Chemical reaction
A chemical process that involves chemicals combining together or splitting apart to form new substances.

Chlorophyll
A green chemical found in the chloroplasts of plant cells.

Chloroplast
The part of a plant cell where photosynthesis takes place. Contains lots of chlorophyll.

Chromatography
A method used to separate out the different coloured solutes in a solution.

Chromosome
A long, coiled up length of DNA.

Cilia
Tiny hair-like structures that stick out from the surfaces of some cells.

Cochlea
A structure in the inner ear. It sends messages about sound vibrations along the auditory nerve.

Combustion
When a fuel burns in oxygen, releasing energy.

Compound
A substance formed when atoms from different elements join together.

Condensing
The change in state of a gas to a liquid.

Glossary

Glossary

Continuous variation

When a feature of an organism can take any value at all within a certain range.

Control variable

A variable in an experiment that is kept the same.

Current (electric)

The flow of charge around a circuit.

Cytoplasm

The jelly-like substance inside a cell where most of its chemical reactions happen.

Decibel

A unit used to measure loudness.

Decomposer

An organism which feeds on the waste and remains of other organisms.

Density

A measure of the 'compactness' of a substance.

Dependent variable

The variable in an experiment that is measured.

Diffusion

When particles spread out and move from an area of high concentration to an area of low concentration.

Digestion

The process in which food is broken down into molecules which can be absorbed and used by the body.

Discontinuous variation

When a feature of an organism can only take certain values.

Disease

Any condition where the workings of the body change for the worse.

Displacement reaction

When a more reactive metal displaces a less reactive metal from its compound.

Dissolving

The process by which a solid mixes with a liquid to form a solution.

Distillation (fractional)

A method for separating a mixture of liquids.

Distillation (simple)

A method for separating a solvent from a solution.

Distilled water

Totally pure water containing no dissolved salts.

DNA

A molecule that is a long list of chemical instructions on how to build an organism.

Drag

Another word for water or air resistance.

Ductility

A property of a material that means it can be drawn into wires.

Ear drum

A structure in the ear which vibrates in response to sound.

Elasticity

A property of a material that means it goes back to its normal shape after being stretched or squashed.

Elastic (strain) energy

The energy an elastic object has when it has been deformed (stretched or squashed).

Electromagnet

A magnet whose magnetic field can be turned on and off with an electric current.

Electron

A small, negatively-charged particle.

Element

A substance that contains only one type of atom, and can't be broken down into any simpler substances.

Embryo

The name given to a developing baby from the time it is a ball of 32 cells until it's a foetus (around 9 weeks).

Emphysema

A disease caused by smoking in which alveoli are destroyed.

Environmental variation

When a feature of an organism is controlled by upbringing or other environmental factors.

Epithelial cell

A cell that is part of the tissue covering the surfaces of your body.

Evaporating

The gradual change in state of a liquid to a gas.

Fair test

A controlled experiment where the only thing that changes is the independent variable.

Fertilisation

The fusion of male and female sex cells during sexual reproduction.

Filtrate

The liquid that has passed through a filter during filtration.

Filtration

The method of separating a solid from a liquid using a filter (like filter paper).

Foetus

The name given to a developing baby from around 9 weeks after fertilisation.

Force

A push or a pull.

Fossil fuels

The fossil fuels are coal, oil and natural gas. They're non-renewable energy resources.

Freezing

The change in state of a liquid to a solid.

Frequency (of sound)

A measure of the pitch of sound. It is the number of complete sound waves that pass a point per second.

Friction

The force that tries to stop objects sliding past each other.

Galaxy

A large collection of stars. The Universe is made of billions of galaxies.

Gamete

Another word for a sex cell.

Gas exchange

The process where oxygen enters the blood from the air and carbon dioxide leaves the blood. Takes place in the lungs.

Glossary

Gene

A short section of a chromosome (and so a short section of DNA).

Global warming

The increase in the temperature of the Earth.

Greenhouse gas

A gas (e.g. carbon dioxide) that traps heat from the Sun in the Earth's atmosphere.

Habitat

The place where an organism lives (e.g. a freshwater pond or hedgerow).

Hazard

Something that has the potential to cause harm (e.g. fire, electricity, etc).

Hertz

A unit used to measure the frequency of sound.

Hooke's Law

A law that says the amount a spring stretches is proportional to the force applied.

Hydrated

A substance containing water.

Hypothesis

A possible explanation for a scientific observation.

Independent variable

The variable in an experiment that is changed.

Indicator

Something that changes colour depending on whether it is in an acid or in an alkali.

Inherited variation

When a feature of an organism is controlled by genes.

Insect

An arthropod that has 6 legs, a 3-part body, 2 pairs of wings and antennae (e.g. a fly).

Insoluble

If a substance is insoluble, this means it will not dissolve in a certain solvent.

Interdependent

Organisms that need each other to survive.

Invertebrate

An animal that has no backbone or spinal column.

Iodine solution

A chemical that turns from brown to blue-black when it comes into contact with starch.

Key

A series of questions used to identify and classify organisms.

Kinetic energy

The energy an object has because it is moving.

Lever

A bar resting on a pivot, used to apply a force on heavy objects.

Light year

A unit used to measure distance in space. It's how far light travels in one year.

Limestone

A naturally-occurring rock mainly formed of calcium carbonate.

Limewater

A colourless solution that goes cloudy when carbon dioxide is bubbled through it.

Luminous

Something that produces light.

Lunar eclipse

When the Earth passes between the Sun and the Moon, stopping the Sun's light from reaching the Moon.

Magnetic field

A region where magnetic materials experience a force.

Malleability

A property of a material that means it can be easily shaped.

Mean (average)

A measure of average found by adding up all the data and dividing by the number of values there are.

Medium

A substance through which waves (such as light and sound) can travel.

Melting

The change in state of a solid to a liquid.

Melting point

The temperature at which a material changes from a solid to a liquid.

Menstrual cycle

A monthly sequence of events that occurs in females from the age of puberty. It involves preparing the uterus to receive a fertilised egg.

Methylene blue

A stain that colours the nuclei of animal cells blue.

Milky Way

The galaxy that contains our Solar System.

Mitochondria

The parts of a cell where the reactions for aerobic respiration take place.

Mixture

Two or more different substances that are mixed up but aren't chemically joined.

Molecule

Two or more atoms joined together.

Moment

The turning effect of a force.

Moneran

A single-celled organism that does not have a nucleus (e.g. bacteria).

Multicellular organism

An organism that is made up of lots of cells.

Neutralisation

When an acid reacts with an alkali to produce a neutral solution of salt and water.

Newton

The unit for force.

Newton meter

The piece of equipment used to measure force.

Non-renewable energy resource

An energy resource that is non-renewable will run out one day. It will run out more quickly the more we use it to generate electricity.

Nucleus

The part of a cell that contains the genes (DNA).

Glossary

Organ
A group of different <u>tissues</u> that work together to perform a function.

Organism
Any living thing.

Ovary
The part of the female reproductive system which produces eggs.

Ovule
Found in the <u>ovary</u> of a flower. Contains the female sex cell.

Ovum
Another word for an egg cell (a female sex cell).

Oxidation
When a substance reacts and combines with oxygen.

Permanent vacuole
The part of a plant cell that is filled with cell sap (a weak <u>solution</u> of sugar and salts).

pH scale
A scale used to measure the strength of acids and alkalis.

Photosynthesis
A chemical process which takes part in every green plant. Light energy is used to convert carbon dioxide and water into glucose and oxygen.

Physical change
A change to a substance that doesn't involve a <u>chemical reaction</u>.

Pivot
The point around which something rotates.

Placenta
An <u>organ</u> that attaches to the wall of the <u>uterus</u> shortly after <u>fertilisation</u>. It allows the blood of the <u>foetus</u> and the mother to get very close together.

Pollen grains
Found in the <u>anther</u> of a flower. Produces the male sex cell.

Pollen tube
A structure that grows out of a <u>pollen grain</u> down into an <u>ovary</u> following <u>pollination</u>.

Pollination
<u>Pollen grains</u> being transferred from a <u>stamen</u> to a <u>stigma</u>.

Population
How many individuals of a particular species there are in a certain place.

Precise result
When all the data is close to the <u>mean</u>.

Prediction
A statement based on a <u>hypothesis</u> that can be tested.

Pressure
How much <u>force</u> is put on a certain area.

Primary consumer
An animal that eats <u>producers</u>.

Producer
An <u>organism</u> that uses the Sun's energy to make its own food.

Product
A chemical you end up with after a <u>chemical reaction</u>.

Protist
A single-celled <u>organism</u> that has a <u>nucleus</u> (e.g. an amoeba).

Quadrat
A square frame enclosing a known area, used to estimate <u>population</u> size.

Random error
A small difference in the results of an experiment caused by things like human error in measuring.

Range
The difference between the smallest and largest values in a set of data.

Reactant
A chemical that you start with in a <u>chemical reaction</u>.

Reactivity series
A list of metals in order of their reactivity towards other substances.

Reduction
A reaction involving a loss of oxygen from a <u>compound</u>.

Refraction
The bending of a wave (e.g. light) as it travels from one <u>medium</u> to another.

Reliable result
A result that is <u>repeatable</u> and <u>reproducible</u>.

Renewable energy resource
An energy resource that is renewable won't run out, no matter how much we use it.

Repeatable result
A result that will come out the same if the experiment is repeated by the same person using the same method and equipment.

Reproducible result
A result that will come out the same if someone different does the experiment, or a slightly different method or piece of equipment is used.

Reptile
A <u>vertebrate</u> that lays eggs on land, has dry scales and is cold-blooded (e.g. a lizard).

Residue
The solid that cannot pass through the filter during <u>filtration</u>.

Resistance
Anything in a circuit that slows down the flow of <u>current</u>.

Respiration
The process of releasing energy from glucose (a sugar). Happens in every cell of every living <u>organism</u>.

Root hair cell
A cell in a plant's roots that absorbs water and minerals from the soil.

Satellite
Something that orbits a planet.

Saturated
A <u>solution</u> that won't dissolve any more <u>solute</u>.

Secondary consumer
An animal that eats <u>primary consumers</u>.

Selective breeding
Where humans try to develop particular varieties of plants or animals with desirable characteristics.

Solar eclipse
When the Moon passes between the Sun and Earth, stopping the Sun's light from reaching Earth.

Soluble
If a substance is <u>soluble</u>, this means it will dissolve in a certain <u>solvent</u>.

Glossary

Solute

A solid that is dissolved in a solvent to form a solution.

Solution

A mixture of a solute and solvent that does not separate out.

Solvent

The liquid that a solute dissolves into to form a solution.

Spectrum

The rainbow effect created when white light gets split up.

Speed

Distance travelled in a certain amount of time.

Sperm

A male sex cell used in animal reproduction.

Stamen

The male part of a flower (consists of an anther and a filament).

Stigma

One of the female parts of a flower. The stigma is the surface that pollen grains attach to before developing a pollen tube at the start of the plant fertilisation.

Stopping distance

The distance covered in the time between a driver first spotting a hazard and the vehicle coming to a complete stop.

Streamlined

Shaped in a way that reduces water or air resistance.

Subliming

The change in state of a substance directly from a solid to a gas.

Sustainable development

Managing the way resources are used, so that the needs of a growing human population can be met without harming the environment.

Systematic error

An error that is consistently made every time throughout an experiment.

Tertiary consumer

An animal that eats secondary consumers.

Testis

The part of the male reproductive system which produces sperm.

Theory

A hypothesis which has been accepted by the scientific community because there is good evidence to back it up.

Thermal decomposition

When a substance breaks down into two or more new substances when heated.

Tissue

A group of similar cells.

Top carnivore

An animal that is not eaten by anything else.

Truth table

A table which links a set of inputs to an output.

Uterus (womb)

The part of the female reproductive system in which a baby grows.

Vaccination

An injection of inactive or dead microorganisms. Causes the white blood cells to produce antibodies, preparing the body for a real infection.

Vacuum

A place where there is nothing at all (i.e. no particles or air).

Variable

A factor in an investigation that can change or be changed (e.g. temperature or concentration).

Variation

Differences between organisms — either between organisms of different species, or between organisms of the same species.

Vertebrate

An animal that has a backbone or spinal column.

Villi

Finger-like projections that line the small intestine. Food molecules are absorbed across them into the blood.

Voltage

The driving force a battery has to push charge around a circuit.

Voltmeter

An instrument used to measure voltage — must be connected in parallel.

Zygote

A fertilised egg cell.

Index

Index

Index and Answers

Answers to Top Tip Questions

Page 35 a) Fewer otters means more pike, which will eat more water beetles.
        b) More pike would mean fewer perch, which could mean fewer water beetles get eaten.

Answers to selected Summary Questions

Summary Questions for Section 6 — Page 54
17) a) magnesium oxide b) carbon dioxide c) sodium chloride d) calcium carbonate
    e) sodium hydroxide
18) a) sodium chloride b) magnesium chloride c) magnesium carbonate

Summary Questions for Section 9 — Page 79
14) 3 A

Summary Questions for Section 10 — Page 89
2)   speed = 10 m ÷ 2 s = 5 m/s
3)   100 m ÷ 15 s = 6.67 m/s. Yes, you can run faster than the bird can fly.
4)   15 minutes = 0.25 hours. 40 mph x 0.25 h = 10 miles.
11)   5 cm ÷ 100 = 0.05 m
      100 N ÷ 0.05 m = 2000 N/m
12)   1 cm
25)   2 m
27)   200 N ÷ 2 m^2 = 100 N/m^2
29)   volume of brick = 10 cm x 10 cm x 3cm = 300 cm^3
      density = 1050 g ÷ 300 cm^3 = 3.5 g/cm^3
30)   mass of liquid = 350 g – 100 g = 250 g
      density = mass ÷ volume = 250 g ÷ 200 cm^3 = 1.25 g/cm^3